MARKING TIME

MARKING TIME

ON THE ANTHROPOLOGY
OF THE CONTEMPORARY

PAUL RABINOW

PRINCETON UNIVERSITY PRESS

PRINCETON AND OXFORD

PUBLISHED BY PRINCETON UNIVERSITY PRESS,
41 WILLIAM STREET, PRINCETON, NEW JERSEY 08540

IN THE UNITED KINGDOM: PRINCETON UNIVERSITY PRESS,
3 MARKET PLACE, WOODSTOCK, OXFORDSHIRE OX20 1SY

LIBRARY OF CONGRESS CATALOGING-IN-PUBLICATION DATA

RABINOW, PAUL.
MARKING TIME : ON THE ANTHROPOLOGY OF THE CONTEMPORARY /
PAUL RABINOW.
P. CM.
INCLUDES BIBLIOGRAPHICAL REFERENCES AND INDEX.
ISBN-13: 978-0-691-13362-1 (HARDCOVER : ALK. PAPER)
ISBN-13: 978-0-691-13363-8 (PBK. : ALK. PAPER)
1. ANTHROPOLOGY—PHILOSOPHY.   2. CONTEMPORARY, THE.   I. TITLE.
GN33.R26 2008
301.01—DC22
2007008388

BRITISH LIBRARY CATALOGING-IN-PUBLICATION DATA IS AVAILABLE

THIS BOOK HAS BEEN COMPOSED IN ITC GALLIARD
WITH TRAJAN DISPLAY

PRINTED ON ACID-FREE PAPER. ∞

PRESS.PRINCETON.EDU

PRINTED IN THE UNITED STATES OF AMERICA

1 3 5 7 9 10 8 6 4 2

✳

CONTENTS

CONTENTS

✸

PREFACE

The phrase "marking time" is a term with several clusters of meaning surrounding it. Among these clusters three in particular are especially pertinent to the mode, tone, and project of this book. (1) The first grouping forms around pauses: a treading between goal-directed actions. This gathering of energy expended in one task and soon to be directed to another after a pause is of course itself an activity. And given the function of treading—catching one's breath, keeping one's head above water—the modality of this first sense of marking time is frequently a reflective one: where should I go next? And how should I get there? (2) A second semantic cluster forms around meanings that are more performative: for example, a keeping of time as a conductor or musician might be expected to do; or an ordering of temporal sequence that a historian might undertake; or the naming of temporal qualities a philosopher might wish to distinguish. Such timely ordering of things is often followed or accompanied by "composing." (3) A third, at present largely virtual cluster, that of an anthropologist of the contemporary, attempts to take elements from the first two, gather them together, while adding an active practice of inquiry of a distinctive sort. *Marking Time* explores some of the dimensions of what that practice entails. This book continues work already accomplished in *Anthropos Today: Reflections on Modern Equipment* devoted to the formation of concepts useful for an anthropology of the contemporary.[1]

The book is itself a punctual intervention marked, as it were, by a particular set of circumstances although its ambitions are of a more general kind. *Marking Time* took shape during a period of research and reflection in the years 2003–2006. There were three distinct, if interconnected, substantive areas of research that occupied and preoccupied me as well as those with whom I was working, thinking, and composing at the time. First and foremost was a continuing engagement with the changing terrain of biotechnology and "postgenomics." An initial challenge was presented by an invitation to conduct anthropological research at Celera Diagnostics in 2003. It seemed to me that if anthropology was going to thrive in the twenty-first century, then it needed to modify its methods of inquiry and its modes of production. The temporality of both, but especially the leisurely, if stressful, duration of the latter, was such that given the pace of change of so many things going on in the contemporary world—from hip hop, to wars, to epidemics, to single nucleotide polymorphism mapping—it would inevitably relegate the discipline to a historical one. Hence the challenge, and thus the exercise, was to conduct a solid research project and to write a book within a year. To do so, certain preliminary and atypical conditions had to be met: it was clear that access, technical familiarity, and a certain type of organization at a specific stage of its enterprise were preconditions. It was also clear that if such work was to succeed it would have to become more collaborative than was traditionally the case in anthropology. This meant not just the ethical collaboration with one's informants and explicit acknowledgment of their contributions, but a different mode of collaboration among the anthropological researchers. While the changes of collaboration in research and publication that had taken place in biology over the previous decades showed that such transformation of scholarly disciplines was possible, it was clear that direct imitation of that model would be misleading. What collaboration might look like in the qualitative human sciences would have to become itself a subject of experimentation. The first exercise designed to meet this challenge, the proof of principle as it were, yielded the book *A Machine to Make a Future: Biotech Chronicles*, co-authored with Talia Dan-Cohen, then an undergraduate at UC Berkeley.[2]

The second project involved what turned out to be a rewarding, multifaceted, and changeable relationship with Roger Brent, director of the Molecular Sciences Institute (MSI), a National Genome Center of Excellence in Computational Biology located in the city of Berkeley (although independent of the university). I had originally intended to conduct research on the MSI's Alpha project, as a timely comparative counterpart and contrast case to that of Celera Diagnostics. Whereas the scientists and business people at Celera Diagnostics were confident in 2003 that the sequencing of the human genome (done in part by their parent company Celera Genomics) opened the door to immediate benefits in terms of identifying major markers for pathological conditions, the Alpha project was based on the premise that biology was not yet a full-fledged science since the field was neither quantitative nor predictive. The intellectually voracious and vivacious Brent and I engaged in many discussions, from which emerged a common agreement that I would not directly carry out research at MSI. Instead we concurred that our energies would be best spent elsewhere: Roger and I should develop a course together that would bring issues of genomics and citizenship into a common frame (we cotaught for three consecutive years from 2003 to 2005). Our free-wheeling and untrammeled discussions led to yet another unexpected swerve in my research interests. Brent convinced me that there was a real and growing danger of new biological threats, and that no even minimally protective bio-defense system existed in the United States (or elsewhere). His insistence on the pressing importance of the threat, and the connections to those working on the problem that he made available, led, with several more twists and turns, to an ongoing research project on the "Global Bio-

Politics of Security" jointly undertaken with professors Stephen Collier and Andrew Lakoff.[3]

The biosecurity interests led me to explore, and to become involved with, the emerging field of synthetic biology. Essentially an attempt to bring engineering standards into molecular biology and organic chemistry, the field broadens and accelerates exciting methods such as the engineered antimalaria molecule artemesinin, isolated from the bark of a Chinese tree, currently being produced in a synthetic form in yeast cells by Jay Keasling and his team at the new Center for Synthetic Biology at UC Berkeley and Lawrence Livermore National Laboratory.[4] The technologies being refined and extended in this and other work, however, also open or advance the possibility of increased capacity and ease in the production of pathogenic agents, either naturally occurring ones, ones worked-over from existing pathogens, or entirely new ones. Beginning in 2006, these concerns and issues—the nature of the objects being produced, the impact of security considerations on the already densely populated worlds of the life sciences, and the possible implications for our understanding of living beings formerly restricted to evolutionary time—constitute the center of my current research.

Finally, whereas synthetic biology clearly continues a line of what has nicely been called "the engineering ideal in America," it also has resonance with early modernist projects, especially that of the Bauhaus, that sought to bring the arts, sciences, crafts, and various technologies into a more fecund relationship with each other, with the dominant political-economic formations of the time, as well as with everyday life.[5] Those themes, as well, are pertinent to my ongoing research. As it happened, during this period I had come to admire the work of the German painter Gerhard Richter. In his own distinctive and particular manner, Richter has provided rich painterly explorations of contemporary media, painting, nature, and aesthetic criticism. An art critic, Peter Osborne, used the phrase "marking time" to characterize Richter's work. Eventually the work, the criticism, and the term seemed connected to and illuminative of what I was attempting to do during this time: ponder and engage with the contemporary forms of *anthropos*, *bios*, and *logos* as they emerged, or faded, or were reformed or simply maintained in motion and in time.

✺

ACKNOWLEDGMENTS

It is a pleasure to acknowledge the large number of people who contribute to making and protecting the vitality of the critical philosophical and anthropological thought and practices as well as scholarly life more broadly. The need for such a form of life is especially important today in a world riven and polluted by anti-intellectualisms, and anti-Enlightenment affect and action, of an ever-increasing variety. Specific debts are owed to authors, living and dead, that community of thinkers which spans generations future and past; such debts are given value through continued reading, discussion, and commentary on their works. Other debts are owed to members of cohort after cohort of talented and challenging students at Berkeley whose curiosity, diversity, and vitality are a splendidly sustaining gift and whose full repayment I hope to continue deferring.

During the gestation period of this book, I have been fortunate to have participated in the imagination, formation, and realization of the Anthroplogy of the Contemporary Research Collaboratory (ARC), www.anthropos-lab.net. We strive to create a space where curiosity and inquiry can thrive and to enjoy ourselves while doing so. And to a surprising extent, we have succeeded. The invitation for others to participate is hereby proffered.

In lieu of detailing the singular encounters that stand behind the following list of names (and a longer list of those unnamed), let me express my deepest gratitude to Roger Brent, Carlo Caduff, Suzanne Calpestri, Stephen Collier, James Faubion,

ACKNOWLEDGMENTS

Tarek el-Haik, Frederic Keck, Christopher Kelty, Arthur Kleinman, Andrew Lakoff, Nicholas Langlitz, George Marcus, Mary Murrell, Peter Osborne, Francis Pisani, Marc Rabinow, Marilyn Rabinow, Tobias Rees, Kaja Silverman, Nikolas Rose, and Meg Stalcup.

MARKING TIME

✳

INTRODUCTION

The anthropology of the contemporary has seemed to me best done by doing it, that is to say, by laying out examples and reflections on those examples. As will be apparent in this book, my inclination is more to show than to tell, in Wittgenstein's sense. At the same time, frequent well-meaning interlocutors, including reviewers of this book in manuscript form, have asked me to explain what I mean by the notion. As a means of acknowledging these requests, while at almost the same time refusing to honor them fully, I offer the following introductory thoughts.

On the Anthropology of the Contemporary

What is the contemporary? The ordinary English-language meaning of the term "the contemporary" is: "existing or occurring at, or dating from, the same period of time as something or somebody else." But there is the second meaning of "distinctively modern in style," as in "a variety of favorite contemporary styles."[1] The first use has no historical connotations, only temporal ones: Cicero was the contemporary of Caesar just as Thelonious Monk was the contemporary of John Coltrane or Gerhard Richter is the contemporary of Gerhard Schroeder. The second meaning, however, does carry a historical connotation and a curious one that can be used to both equate and differentiate the contemporary from the modern. It is that marking that is pertinent to the project at hand. Just as one can take up the "modern" as an ethos and not a period, one can take it up as a moving ratio. In that perspective, tradition and modernity are not opposed but paired: "tradition is a moving image of the past, opposed not to modernity but to alienation."[2] *The contemporary is a moving ratio of modernity, moving through the recent past and near future in a (nonlinear) space that gauges modernity as an ethos already becoming historical.*

There are three guiding ideas here. First, the contemporary is not an epochal term. For much of the twentieth century various movements that labeled themselves modernist were fixated on "the new." And the identification of the new was frequently tied to a more or less explicit philosophy of history in which the new was usually better or at least the result of an inevitable motion. In parallel with the culture concept, it was held that eras or epochs had a unity that tied diverse domains of practice and experience together into a whole that was, if not seamless, at least coherent. But as the faith and belief in such ontological entities (culture, epochs, progress) has been challenged, it has become apparent to some that understanding modernism and "the modern" required some critical distance from its own assumptions. This distance could be achieved through historical work that showed the contingency, inconsistencies, differential strata underlying the surface unity, and the like. Or it could be achieved through a conscious abandonment of epochal thinking, including as many of its presuppositions as could plausibly be reexamined. In this light, it is clear that in many domains old and new elements do coexist in multiple configurations and variations. Thus, if one no longer assumes that the new is what is dominant, to use Raymond Williams's distinction, and that the old is somehow essentially residual, then the question of how older and newer elements are given form and worked together, either well or poorly, becomes a significant site of inquiry.[3] I call that site the contemporary.

For example, the fact that the human genome has been mapped, and population differences at the molecular level identified, does not mean that older understandings of race disappear in the light of this new knowledge. But neither does it not mean that all of the older understandings of what constitutes difference undergo a total transformation. Rather, the problem for an anthropology of the contemporary is to inquire into what is taking place without deducing it beforehand. And that requires sustained research, patience, and new concepts, or modified old ones. The purpose is not destruction or deconstruction but a reevaluation; its goal is not reform or revolution but rather a type of remediation.

Once again, observers as well as the practitioners of the contemporary are not principally concerned with "the new" or with distinguishing themselves from tradition. Rather, they are intrigued by the operations of the distinction modern/contemporary as the clustered elements and stylized configurations of the modern are observed in the process of declusterings, reconfigurations, and different stylizations or made to do so. As I have argued in *Anthropos Today*, this mode of observation and practice is one of secession rather than of the avant-garde or its presumed opposite, the neoconservative.[4] Secession marks, observes, and stylizes in a recursive manner.

Second, there is a difference between emphasizing reproduction and emphasizing emergence. This difference holds for the subjects in the world as much as for analysts. Most of anthropology and significant portions of the other social sciences concentrate on how society or culture reproduces itself (and this includes many models of "change") through institutions, symbolic work, power relations, or the cunning of reason. And there

3

is much to be said in favor of this mode of analysis. But it has become apparent that there are other phenomena present today, as no doubt there have been at other times in other places, that are emergent. That is to say, phenomena that can only be partially explained or comprehended by previous modes of analysis or existing practices. Such phenomena, it follows, require a distinctive mode of approach, an array of appropriate concepts, and almost certainly different modes of presentation.

Third, by "anthropology" I do not mean ethnography understood as a practice developed to analyze a specific type of object—the culture and/or society of *ethnoi*—so as to contribute to a specific genre, the monograph (or journal article). Nor do I mean philosophic anthropology in the nineteenth-century European sense, whether materialist or idealist, whose object was the nature or essence of Mankind and whose genre was the treatise. Nor do I intend the mixed forms of research and writing that proliferated around this unstable object, *l'homme*, which attempted, while continually failing, to bring the transcendental and the empirical into a stable relationship, so powerfully described by Michel Foucault in *The Order of Things*, even if Foucault himself was tempted for a time to overcome and stabilize things, an attempt he eventually abandoned. Rather, I take the object of anthropological science (*Wissenschaft*) to be the dynamic and mutually constitutive, if partial and dynamic, connections between figures of *anthropos* and the diverse, and at times inconsistent, branches of knowledge available during a period of time; that claim authority about the truth of the matter; and whose legitimacy to make such claims is accepted as plausible by other such claimants; as well as the power relations within which and through which those claims are produced, established, contested, defeated, affirmed, and disseminated.

Thus, taken as an object domain, contemporary anthropology is neither as broad as traditional ethnography nor as grand as classic philosophic anthropology nor as ambitious as the human sciences. This narrowing of scope has some advantages: there are good reasons to accept the claim (*sic*) that a restricted form of anthropology refers to an actual object domain in the present whose recent past, near future, and emergent forms can be observed. Of course, one can observe and analyze that object domain in diverse manners. One challenge, the one at hand in this book, is to contribute to orientations that would mark a means of producing anthropological knowledge anthropologically.[5]

Marking Time is neither a standard monograph nor a traditional collection of essays. It is not a monograph in that it does not have a single guiding argument, clearly stated at the outset, and rigorously held to task in the ensuing chapters. Neither is it simply a book of essays in that the chapters that follow are not previously published pieces grouped together and unified by having the same author. Rather, there are connections between the chapters; these connections have a pliable logic that readers may discern could have been assembled differently, producing a different flow and effect. One might say that the mode of assemblage is a contemporary one. Finally, and to the point, the book's chapters share both a temporality and a historicity; they were written during a period of labor, work, and exploration within a particular problem space. The contours and dynamics of that (nonmetric) space became clearer during the course of a series of orienting experiments in form.[6] Those experiments were all calibrated, with varying degrees of precision and success, toward designing inquiry. Design is a dynamic and collaborative practice about which there is more to be said and which currently forms a topic of intense collaboration and future work.[7] For the present, however, the first question at hand is: what is inquiry? And thus readers eager for definitions and guidelines will now receive some, with at least a preliminary rationale for why they are being presented in their current form.

Inquiry

Following John Dewey and Richard McKeon, we can define a term as a word + a concept + a referent. Thus the same word, for example, "philosophy" or "anthropology," can take its place in different terms. There is a frequent confusion between a word and a term. At the outset, therefore, it is appropriate to highlight some of the key concepts at work in the terms used in this work.

The general issue of how to characterize anthropological inquiry has been a surprisingly underexplored subject. Given this gap and given my formation and inclinations, the tradition of pragmatic and nominalist thinking was the place I was likely to find conceptual help. John Dewey's 1938 magnum opus (written at age eighty), *Logic: The Theory of Inquiry*, proved invaluable in providing a general orientation as well as specific concepts albeit with certain critical limitations.[8] The concept and practice of inquiry were central to John Dewey's life work. He published a large number of studies on the topic, both highly technical and more popular, spanning a period from his collected *Essays in Experimental Logic* (1903, 1916) to the 1940s. The pertinent conceptual orientation of Dewey's term inquiry is taken up in the subsequent section.

The main limitations of his approach for anthropological inquiry, it seems to me, are found in his inability to leave the practices, skills, and narrative forms of traditional philosophy behind, even though time and time again he explicitly advocated doing so.[9] Dewey's practice remains abstract even though his rhetorical aim was to move the reader away from such a traditional mode of thinking and writing. One might well expect that a thinker who insisted with force and conviction that the task and challenge of contemporary philosophy was to overcome traditional philosophy's insistence on certainty, abstraction, and timelessness would himself seek to integrate the analysis of substantive topics — specific problem situations — into the very warp and woof of his practice. But in Dewey's case one would be disappointed. He remains a traditional philosopher *malgré lui*. Dewey (1859–1952), like Martin Heidegger (1889–1976), simply did not concern himself with the genealogical details of the "merely ontic," any more than did Dewey's contemporary analytic philosophers (Russell, Moore, Wittgenstein, and others), who perfected the technique of using thin, school-masterly examples to draw large philosophic conclusions. In sum, Dewey's treatise lacks any sustained attempt to instantiate the analytic process he advocated.[10]

Fundamentally, Dewey is not nominalist enough. He writes despite himself as if his objects were atemporal. He does not provide any historical contextualization to locate and delimit his key terms, such as "breakdown," "situation," and "reconstruction." The danger in this practice is that one risks ontologizing these categories.[11] Various other thinkers, such as Reinhart Koselleck with his "history of concepts," developed a form of inquiry that would have been consistent with the overall project of Dewey's logic but would have entailed a different set of intellectual skills. Although it would be of interest to explore the historical conditions in which Dewey's terms, practices, and modes were formed, such an undertaking obviously is neither my intent nor my interest here. Rather, I am trying to appropriate conceptual tools that had been forged for certain problems, and to refashion them in the hope that they will provide analytic purchase for different problems.

Elements

Despite the limitations of Dewey's approach, his claims about the nature of inquiry provide helpful orientation points for a renewed practice of inquiry. As an introductory device, I propose a series of Deweyan claims about the nature of inquiry.[12]

1. "*Inquiry begins in an indeterminate situation*," Dewey argues that inquiry is a continuous, reiterative process. Inquiry is not restricted to scientific or traditional philosophic questions per se but is involved with ordinary life as well as larger political and cultural issues. Hence inquiry begins midstream, always already embedded in a situation, one both settled and unsettled. Inquiry moves through the process of inquiry itself to other situations and other problems, themselves both stabilized and troubled. Thus, it is perfectly appropriate to begin with tentative parameters of a situation to be inquired into and tentative understandings of what is at stake.

2. "*and not only begins in it but is controlled by its specific qualitative nature*." There are situations that may reach a determined state rapidly and others where it is not possible to tell before the inquiry is well under way whether, and in what manner, and for how long, it will take to move beyond a first loose state to one in which both the situation and its determinants become clearer, more determinate. Thus, to claim to know beforehand precisely what one is going to do, or to find, as grant proposals demand, would constitute bad method, poor logic, and falsely disciplined inquiry. Or, more accurately, it seems to me, run the risk of not doing inquiry at all.

3. "*Inquiry, as the set of operations by which the situation is resolved (settled or rendered determinate)*: Inquiry is not an empiricism in the sense of discovering what is out there as if it were transparent and passive, simply waiting to be represented. Nor is inquiry theory driven in the sense that a situation can be reduced to a particular case of a more general theory (this is in part because one cannot know beforehand what the status of one's concepts are or whether the initial situation has any unity). Inquiry is a form of constructivism or operationalism: Dewey means this in a common-sense way (problems and thought require action to exist) and in a more technical sense (since inquiry arises within

a problematic and indeterminate situation, the inquirer is not outside the situation, nor is she in a position such that she could construct something that was not to a degree present already). Hence, operations are necessarily part of the indeterminate situation once it is taken up by an inquiry.

4. *"has to discover and formulate the conditions which describe the problem at hand."* By "discover the conditions" Dewey "indicates" that inquiry is situated and its goal is to isolate something in the world that is causing or occasioning effects. By "formulate," Dewey is making a strong claim, one that runs throughout his work, that the giving of form (whether discursive, logical, artistic, scientific, political, and the like) is a primary task in living in general as well as in specific practices themselves conditioned by traditions and habits. Form giving is thus an essential goal of "describing" a problem and of shaping an inquiry. Description rather than explanation is the goal, but description is not a naïve act but one that can arise only within a process of inquiry that is engaged in one or another type of form making.

5. *"For they are the conditions to be 'satisfied' and [are] the determinants of 'success.'"* Since the problem lies in the situation and the situation is conditioned by various factors, it is only through discovering and giving form to elements that are already present that the inquiry can proceed. Hence the process involves staying in the midst of the things of the world and transforming them in specific ways so as to give them the kind of determinative form that can be known.

6. *"Since these conditions are existential, they can be determined only by observational operations; the operational character of observation being clearly exhibited in the experimental character of all scientific determination of data."* Inquiry is experimental in its form giving. Hence the interest of an experiment is its ability not to represent a preexisting situation nor to construct an entirely new one but rather reiterated and controlled adjustment. There are

no abstract criteria available that one could deploy beforehand to judge whether the experiment has succeeded or not: the reason for this is that *"the conditions are existential."*

7. *"The conditions discovered, accordingly, in and by operational observation, constitute the conditions of the problem with which further inquiry is engaged; for the data, on this view, are always data of some specific problem and hence are not given ready-made to an inquiry but are determined in and by it."* That is to say, a successful inquiry will arise in, work through, and seek form for concrete contexts. Obviously this claim does not mean that there are no generalities in the world or in knowledge, only that it is improper to neglect the fact that they arose from a set of operations and observations that were partially determined by and partially determinative of a prior indeterminate situation.

8. *"As the problem progressively assumes definite shape by means of repeated acts of observation, possible solutions suggest themselves."* These solutions may be practical solutions to a problem in ordinary life; they may be scientific solutions to a defined problem of an experimental form; they may be artistic solutions to a given challenge of artistic practice, etc. Hence, problems and solutions are terms that are joined in practice and in that sense coproductive.

9. *"The process of reasoning is the elaboration of them."* The solution to a particular problem consists in a series of steps whose particularities are not known before those steps are undertaken. The observation and reflection on the process can be called reason as long as one is clear that reason is neither a faculty of mind nor a quality of the things themselves, but rather a distinctive mode of taking up the practice of inquiry.

In retrospect, Dewey's attempt to make his logic applicable to any problem, anywhere, and anytime both gives it its power and constitutes its core blind spot.[13] In parallel with what anthropologists used to call the "ethnographic present," one might say that Dewey wrote in the "philosophic present." Of course, situating his thought historically does not discredit the insights and analytic tools he forged; it only shows that the situations Dewey analyzed were, at least in part, historically specific. Today we can see that Dewey's pragmatism was only partial and that his adjacency was insufficiently conceptualized to serve the anthropologist of the contemporary without modification.

✺

THE LEGITIMACY OF THE
CONTEMPORARY

The only question that remains is the sense in which
science [Wissenschaft] gives "no" answer, and whether
or not science [Wissenschaft] might yet be of some use
to the one who puts the question correctly.
            —Max Weber[1]

The initial mapping and sequencing of the human and
other genomes during the course of the 1990s was an
event; in its wake almost everyone seems to agree that
we are on the verge of something momentous and extravagant.
In English, "verge" means the boundary beyond which something happens or changes. The sequence, it is true, is only one
in a larger series of recent bravura, techno-scientific accomplish-
ments that individually and in an accumulative fashion raise a
host of unsettling and unsettled issues ranging from the scientific, to the ontological, to the ethical, to the political. Today,
there is ferocious contestation over whether these achievements
are: (a) transgressing a boundary whose integrity we must respect; or (b) crossing over a threshold leading to unforeseen encounters and challenges; or (c) simply moving from one farmer's
field to the next (the original meaning of verge) and thereby ba-

sically issues of private property and the commons. But how is one to decide where one is? And where one is going?

To put the question another way: how is one to decide: what difference does today introduce with respect to yesterday? That formulation, of course, is how Michel Foucault, two decades ago, rephrased the question—"What is Enlightenment?"—posed by Immanuel Kant two centuries earlier.[2] The core claim of this is that to better understand the question, the stakes, and hopefully the way to proceed—Kant's famous "exit," "*Ausgang*," from immaturity—we require something like an anthropology of the contemporary.

A variant of the question Foucault posed, albeit in a quite different form, can be found in the great work of Hans Blumenberg, especially his magnum opus, *The Legitimacy of the Modern Age*. Arguing against Martin Heidegger, Carl Schmitt, Karl Löwith, and others who saw in modern forms of self-assertion and reason a dangerous nihilism or self-deluding attempts to overcome Christianity while only furthering its deepest essence through the process of secularization, Blumenberg's book is a plea and justification, an apologia, an *éloge*, for a distinctive space of inquiry, one that is affirmative of a modern ethos. Blumenberg's legitimacy of modernity is as well a variant of the legitimacy of the contemporary, a call to remain open to the present, against narratives of decline, disaster, and other forms of closure. For Blumenberg, the difference that constitutes modernity's legitimacy, and possibly an *Ausgang*, is a critical one: once one finds oneself on the verge of casting the present in epochal terms (as a historical totality), as we have become accustomed to do since the nineteenth century, one must cease and desist; once one finds oneself attempting to answer the old metaphysical and theological problems with which so much Western philosophy is still enmeshed, one should pause and attempt to ask, with more precision, what is the problem that makes a difference now? By so doing, it might be possible to affirm a form of conceptual curiosity and appropriate self-assertion about and within the contemporary. Dare to know! But only those things that can be known.

Odo Marquard, in his *Schwierigkeiten mit der Geschichtsphilosophie*, carries these reflections forward by questioning how we could think about change without a philosophy of history, and produce an anthropology without a fixed conception of Man.[3] These questions are precisely the domain of an anthropology of reason and/or an anthropology of the contemporary. Such an anthropology, however, would explore more heterogeneous territory than the largely conceptual terrain to which thinkers like Blumenberg and Marquard restrict themselves. Today, *anthropos* is in question; this questioning has multiple dimensions to it. One of those dimensions, but only one, is the rise of a powerful new set of sciences. Thus, it is unequivocally the case that the *logos* of *bios* is currently in the process of rapid transformation. A central question before us today therefore is: given a changing biology, what *logos* is appropriate for *anthropos*? And how should that *logos* be practiced so as to increase our capacities without intensifying the myriad relations of brutalization that are so pervasive unto our times? Brutalization: the act of treating something viciously, without care. The older meaning refers to the state of existence of animals and lower races; the contemporary meaning refers to how these living beings are treated by the civilized and humane. And the consequences for those doing so.

2000: Drosophila Lessons

There is little doubt that the March 24, 2000, issue of *Science* entitled *The Drosophila Genome* marks a threshold. The humble fruit fly has been the twentieth century's organism of choice for studying genetics. Its centrality has persisted from its early fame at Columbia University, where it was chosen as a model organism in part because its reproductive habits fit the academic calendar, up to the present, when a hybrid consortium of public university labs (especially Berkeley) and the controversial biotechnology company Celera Genomics, chose Drosophila as a demonstration project for their genome mapping strategies. Celera did so in part to prove to its competitors (especially the U.S.-government-funded university/philanthropy consortium mapping the human genome) the power of its sequencing approach. The Drosophila sequence was also presented as a gift to science (free CD-ROMs are available), a token of this early twenty-first-century triumph of utter technological power. More has been learned in the three years about Drosophila genetics than had been painstaking accumulated in the previous seventy-five. Thus, the *Drosophila Genome* issue of *Science* contains much to ponder for geneticists and for nongeneticists alike.[4] And, of course, it was not long before *Science* published its special issue on *The Human Genome*.

One of the elder statesmen of genetics, the Nobel Prize winner Sydney Brenner, in a trenchant summary piece preceding the the *Drosophila Genome* insert, aptly entitled "The End of the Beginning," brilliantly frames the significance of the current conjuncture in genetics. Brenner, himself the leader of the project to map the worm, *C. Elegans*, opens his article by observing that "In classical experimental genetics, we could not assert the existence of a wild-type gene until a mutant version with an altered function had been isolated. But," he continues, "if one asked how many genes were required to make a bacteriophage or a bacterium or a fly or a mouse, no answer could be given."[5] Classical geneticists could never have produced a *Drosophila Genome* special issue because, although they had developed techniques to isolate and map "genes," classical genetics had no concept equivalent to what is today called "a genome." Consequently, it is not surprising that no answer was given to a question that could not be scientifically posed: what is a genome?

Just as "genes" and "genomics" are not the same thing, so too "genes" and "DNA" are not the same thing. In fact, DNA plays an intermediary role between genes and genomes. The major shift that eventuated in the invention, discovery, and mapping of genomes during the 1990s arguably began with the shift from "genes" to "DNA." Following the discoveries of the 1950s and 1960s in which the fundamentals of the double helix and genetic code were painstakingly unraveled, the 1970s and 1980s saw the invention of a series of technologies devoted to manipulating DNA (regardless of its function); the most important were DNA sequencing, cloning DNA in bacteria, and the polymerase chain reaction (PCR, also referred to as "in vitro" cloning), a technique that enabled the rapid, efficient, and inexpensive production of large quantities of specific DNA sequences. With the invention of PCR at Cetus Corporation, a scarcity of DNA available for experimentation turned into a bounty of DNA available for experimentation.[6] The 1970s and 1980s were also the decades during which the material conditions of production of truth in molecular biology, biochemistry, and genetics were undergoing, not coincidentally, equally significantly changes. These were the decades of the emergence of the biotechnology industry—the end of an elite, artisan, craft culture in biology, even in the recently forged specialty of molecular biology, and its rapid replacement with a distinctive type of heavily machine-mediated, costly mode of quasi-industrial production, replete with a much larger and more functionally diverse labor force including computer technicians, lawyers, chief executive officers, and advertising agencies. Joining the crowded world of DNA was another new player, bioethicists. While companies such as Genentech, Cetus, and Biogen were shaping the field, the university world was itself moving significantly closer to this new industrial mode of operation. By 1989 it was daring but plausible for the U.S. National Institutes of Health and Department of Energy (involved in radiation research since the dropping of the atomic bombs in Japan) to announce a Human Genome Initiative, designed to map (and eventually sequence) the human genome—defined ambiguously as the total complement of DNA in a human cell—and thereby it was proclaimed to bring health and prosperity, eventually, to many.[7]

Today, fourteen years later, a series of genomes have been mapped through massively funded, international, industry-government-university-philanthropy consortia. Many consequences and questions flow along with this achievement. Prominent among them is a contemporary rethinking of the "gene." Scientifically speaking, "genes" are not what they used to be. Brenner ruefully remarks, "Old geneticists knew what they were talking about when they used the term 'gene,' but it seems to have been corrupted by modern genomics to mean any piece of expressed sequence." Instead of the misleading and anachronistic term "gene," Brenner proposes to substitute the term "genetic locus" to indicate "either an open reading frame or a site to map mutations."[8] An open reading frame is "a DNA sequence that potentially can be translated into protein." It should be no surprise to learn that proteomics companies are appearing, and calls for inventories of proteins are increasingly mentioned as vital.

The full impact of this conceptual shift in our understanding of living beings has not achieved an adequate place in public understanding given all the attention that the media has lavished on the "gene for" this, that, and the other thing, as well as such hot-button issues, seemingly rife with epochal significance, as "patenting life" (remember that), "cloning humans," and "genetically modified foods." In fact, the gene for this-that-and-the-other-thing should probably be seen as one of the last triumphs of what Brenner calls "classical genetics." It is eminently worthwhile to underscore Brenner's point that locating genes is not the same thing as mapping or sequencing genomes. Furthermore, those engaged in the latter enterprise are perfectly clear that these stages are only an initial step in understanding genomes. Once the genomes are mapped and sequenced and once the basic proteomic cataloging work is accomplished, the functional biology will only just have begun. Brenner observes that these maps are static. None of the information in them as it is currently collected tells us when genes are switched on and off and for how long. Such information, Brenner observes, is "absolutely essential [   ] because in complex organisms, evolution does not proceed by enlarging the protein inventory but by modulating the expression of genes."

In an equally stunning summing up of the state of comparative genomics in the year 2000, the head of the Berkeley *Drosophila* project, Gerald Rubin, and a host of coauthors presented the first overviews of the "Comparative Genomics of the Eukaryotes."[9] Rubin and colleagues set out a series of initial insights that are in many ways counterintuitive and quite surprising. Let me just list some of them: (1) *Drosophila* has a proteome only twice the size of that of yeast. And, despite the large differences between fly and worm in terms of development and morphology, "they use a core proteome of similar size."[10] (2) Complexity and number of genes are not directly correlated "There is presently no practical way to quantify differences in biological complexity between two organisms" (3) "Genes with similar functional assignment in the Gene Ontology classification do not appear to be clustered in the genome." (4) Human disease genes. A list was compiled of 289 genes that are mutated, altered, amplified, or deleted in a diverse set of human disease and searched for similar diseases in the three genomes. Of these 289 human genes, 177 (61 percent) appear to have an ortholog in *Drosophila*. Of the human cancer genes surveyed, 68 percent appear to have *Drosophila* orthologs. Numerous orthologs of neurological genes are also found in the *Drosophila* genome. (5) *Drosophila's* utility as an experimental site will only increase. Many of the human disease genes are found in only a single copy in the fly, and hence there is less ambiguity about their function. Gene manipulation in the fly is easy and can demonstrate possible genetic therapeutic approaches. We anticipate the increased use of such 'humanized' fly models.[11] (6) "The human genome, with 80,000 or so genes, is likely to be an amplified version of a very much smaller genome, and its core proteome may not be much larger than that of the fly or worm; that is, the more complex attributes of human beings are achieved using largely the same molecular components. The evolution of additional complex attributes is essentially an organizational one: a matter of novel interactions that derive from the temporal and spatial segregation of fairly similar components."

Notice, please, that in the year 2000 Rubin's estimate of the number of human genes was off by at least an order of magnitude. In the fall of 2003, Affymetrix, a Silicon Valley company, announced a gene chip that would monitor expression patterns of all the genes in the human genome. This task was facilitated by the fact that the number of genes to monitor is about one-third of what was expected. However, as Stephen Fodor, the founder and CEO of Affymetrix, told me in September 2003, since the coding regions of the genome represent only about 2 percent of the DNA, there is much work left to be done on what the rest of the genome is doing. Of course since then the discovery of interference RNA has led to a more precise understanding of splicing processes and a burgeoning set of startup companies.

Scientific knowledge, even its fundamental truths, changes. Accepting that condition is what makes science a difficult and challenging vocation. Those not ready to live within such instability, with its pleasures and frustrations, as Weber taught us, should seek other work.

The Future of Human Nature

Germany's most distinguished philosopher, Jürgen Habermas, in his manifesto, *The Future of Human Nature*, boldly answers the call to come to terms with recent events taking place in the life sciences as well as in ethics. In his book, rather surprisingly he does not take up the life sciences at all. He chooses to cast the question of ethics as a dilemma formulated by the following rhetorical question:"Do we want to treat the categorically new possibility of intervening in the human genome as an increase in freedom that requires normative *regulation* — or rather as self-empowerment for transformations that depend simply on our preferences and do not require any *self-limitation?*"[12]

The question is a rhetorical one in the sense that the way Habermas posed it, he has already answered it. He devotes the core of his short book to making arguments in favor of banning intervention in the human genome (now and forever). Habermas's conclusion, although not the reasons for it, is basically the same one as that of Frances Fukuyama and Leon Kass, both formerly members of President George W. Bush's National Commission on Bio-Ethics, which is to point out that similar intellectual and moral positions can be held by people spanning the political spectrum. Although I disagree with this position, there is no doubt that it must receive the attention of anthropologists today for, when all is said and done, what is at stake is an understanding of—and an attitude toward—*anthropos* and *logos*.

There are a series of claims, both explicit and implicit, in Habermas's question. He appears to posit two human natures: a biological one that he equates with the genome (although one is told nothing about what he considers the genome to be), and a human nature exterior to the genome as well as qualitatively different from it. Identity, the capacity for healthy human relations, and individual self-worth all depend on the genome remaining untouched in a state of nature; it is only when that con-

20

dition of inviolability is met that we can be assured that our autonomy and freedom are protected, or at least the conditions are in place for it to be so. On the face of it, each of these claims is dubious and far from self-evident. As anthropologists, however, we should take no native claims as absurd a priori—after all, our discipline has spent years unraveling the complex semiotics that make a speech act possible and coherent whereby an Amazonian tribesman claims to be a parakeet. Here, as with the Bororo, we seem to be dealing with a worldview. Or at least that is how anthropology has traditionally cast such matters.

Habermas's book is a social fact. It is a part of a distinctive contemporary moral landscape. This landscape is not external (as Habermas seems to assume) to the current reconfiguration of *anthropos;* bio-ethics and biosciences are in a relationship— often a discordant one, but still a relationship. Thus, it is perfectly legitimate for an anthropologist to map the reconfigurations of the *logos* of *anthropos* and thus to analyze Habermas's intervention as part of contemporary affairs.

In terms of cultural history, there is nothing opaque about Habermas's position; it is essentially a lightly modified version of the nineteenth-century understanding, widespread in German philosophic circles, that technology and nature are ontologically separate realms that must be kept epistemologically and morally distinct. In the Kantian tradition, nature is the realm of necessity and reason the realm of freedom. Although Habermas emphatically affirms that distinction, he also introduces a variant of Hegelianism: "Subjectivity, being what makes the human body a soul-possessing receptacle of the spirit, is itself constituted through inter-subjective relations to others. The individual self will only emerge through the course of social externalization, and can only be stabilized with the network of undamaged relations of mutual recognition" (34).

Habermas states and restates his position in a remarkable variety of ways: perhaps he is not yet sure which formulation is the best one; perhaps he recognizes that the formulations themselves are unstable and do not bear much intellectual scrutiny. The advances of molecular biology appear to be making it possible to intervene in fundamental regulatory mechanisms of living beings. One must beware, however, as this capacity may lead to places one does not normatively want to go. We need critical limits because there is a danger of "obliterating the boundary between persons and things." In the light of this diagnosis, Habermas's basic imperative follows logically: "This kind of intervention should be exercised only over things, not persons" (13). Although this imperative sounds like Kant, old Kant was just a shade less categorical than Habermas. Kant says: "So act as to treat humanity, whether in thine own person or in that of any other, in every case as an end withal, never as a means only."[13] In my opinion, Kant's "only" adds a crucial space of reflection and action.

Bio-ethics: The Question Concerning Humanism

Habermas's schema does not seem to have a category of "living beings." Thus, apparently it would be normatively permissible to intervene in the genomes of Drosophila, mice, yeast, and chimps—and to treat them like things. Granted, Habermas does express some ambivalence on this point. The tone of the following sentence (and others like it) is clearly one of disapproval: "What was hitherto 'given' in organic nature, and could at most be 'bred,' now shifts to the realm of artifacts and their production."[14] Habermas speaks of "ruthless intrusion" into nature, although there is no evident reason why he chooses to call these practices "ruthless" and not "caring." It is striking—and not innocent—that Habermas invokes the following example: "It is true that, just like the rationalization of agriculture, which was rationalized according to business management principles, the technological equipment and up-grading of a health-care system dependent on pharmaceutical businesses and medical machinery have been prone to crisis" (46). The "prone to crisis" phrase is a strange one, as if precapitalist peasant agriculture or socialist agriculture and medical systems were not prone to crisis. It is impossible not to hear uncanny echoes here of Heidegger's claim that there is no difference between mechanized agriculture and the concentration camps. For these German philosophers at least, admixtures of technology and nature remain morally unbearable and, perhaps for that reason, unthinkable.

Habermas is most concerned with establishing moral boundaries to protect an endangered humanity. Habermas basically does seem willing, however reluctantly, to accept technological intervention in external nature: "From a life-world perspective, however, our attitude changes as soon as this extension of our technological control crosses the line between 'outer' and 'inner' nature" (23). The foundation but not the essence of that "inner nature" seems to be genomic. Thus: "Up until now both the secular thought of European modernity and religious belief could proceed on the assumption that the genetic endowment of the newborn infant, and thus the initial organic conditions for its future life history, lay beyond any programming and deliberate manipulation on the part of other persons" (13). Although this claim is historically dubious, the message is clear. It is debatable because the largely secular eugenics movement of both the right wing and the left wing certainly wanted to intervene in the genetic endowment of the newborn infant. What these movements understood by "genetic endowment" has taken on incompatible meanings over the course of the last century. The public health movement certainly sought to intervene deliberately and in a regulatory fashion in "the initial organic conditions" of life.

Habermas identifies a slippery slope so dear to Anglophone ethicists and philosophers and adds to it a bit of apocalyptic

23

rhetoric from old Europe. "Once you start to instrumentalize human life, once you start to distinguish between life worth living, and life not worth living, you embark on a course where there is no stopping point" (19). There is another kind of analytic slippage here, one between an instrumentalizing of human life, on the one hand, and deciding on which lives are worth living, on the other. Surely it is possible for someone to decide (alone, with their family, friends, doctors, pastoral care givers) that their life is no longer worth living without that decision leading to the concentration camps. To claim otherwise is to retreat from the "demands of the day," as Weber put it. Regardless, for Habermas, the remedy is clear. "The abstract morality of reason proper to subjects of human rights is itself sustained by a prior *ethical self-understanding of the species*, which is shared by all *moral persons*" (40). For many of us, this statement occasions fear and trembling, shock and awe, and above all anger. The idea that there is an a priori ethical self-understanding of the species, and that if you don't share it with Habermas you are not a moral person, is, to use one of his terms, repugnant.

There is much to be said about all of this. Here I point out that, as we are no longer in the nineteenth century, the resurrection of this old stance picques the curiosity of an anthropologist of the contemporary. Habermas activates old concepts to encompass and secure the present: precisely his definition of neoconservatism, one he used polemically in other debates. An anthropologist of the contemporary is attentive to the issue of "What difference does today make with regard to yesterday?" This position by no means rejects the use of older concepts; quite the contrary, but it does attempt to look at them anew, to refashion them in light of new elements and new problems. The ethos of the contemporary contrasts with that of the modern; it is not fascinated with the new per se but concerned with the emergence and articulation of forms within which old and new elements take on meanings and functions. Today, there is no doubt that one site of such problems is: how might we forge a way of life that does not make a sharp and brutal separation between what used to be called nature and culture?

Nature

Georges Canguilhem, in an acerbic article entitled "Nature dénaturée et nature naturante" [Nature denatured and naturalizing nature] provides a stern pedagogical lesson to those who hold sentimental views of nature's purity. Canguilhem's article was written at a time (1976) when ecology was gaining a momentary prominence on the French political scene. Canguilhem observes that Western history has seen sporadic waves of protest against the putative "denaturation of human life in both its means and its ends" putatively caused by technico-economic practices. The common denominator of all such protests is an affect of regret, a deploring of the loss of an imagined, unmediated contact with *"cette sorte d'absolue originaire, de référence indépassable, dont il est rêvé sous le nom de Nature"* [that originary absolute, essential reference, about which people dream under the name of nature].[15] For Canguilhem, such a position is scientifically absurd, although he admits, not without a certain self-satisfaction dear to secular French thinkers, that the position as well as its associated emotion could well be theologically coherent.[16]

All techniques are artificial; this banality, however, does not imply that techniques are metaphysically distinct from or opposed to nature in any ontological way. For example, if agricultural techniques are to succeed, they must be "rigorously conditioned by the very nature of animal and vegetable functions of growth and multiplication" (78). This stricture applies to whatever form of technology is at issue, be it that of peasants, industrial agriculturalists, or organic farmers. *"L'homme a longtemps*

25

semé ce qu'il avait récolté sans l'avoir fait pousser" [For a long time, man has harvested that which he has sown without having made it grow] (79). One can intervene in multiple ways with organic things, but the things themselves must have the potential to integrate those changes if the results are to be anything approaching what those applying the technology had sought to bring forth. Certain interventions will do nothing or produce loss; others will increase yield or produce unexpected results. Technology can be seen as a mode of revealing potentials, not essences.

Canguilhem draws two major conclusions from this principle. First: "Scientifically speaking, denaturation is meaningless. Technically speaking, denaturation means a change in use. No use is inscribed in the nature of things. The very first use of a thing is its denaturation" (84).[17] Or, said another way: "It is certain that one does not denature nature in orienting its powers towards effects that are not the usual ones" (85).[18] We are only just beginning to learn again how polyvalent and overdetermined organic systems already are; we know very little about their limits. Biotechnological interventions will surely teach us more. Such knowledge, like all knowledge, carries with it risks (87).[19]

Security, Danger, Risk

When discussing risk there is always a definitional question to be addressed, as there are many different ways to approach the topic. Here I adopt the distinctions proposed by Niklas Luhmann in his book, *Risk: A Sociological Theory*. Luhmann asserts that the world "knows no risks, for it knows neither distinctions, nor expectations, nor evaluations, nor probabilities—*unless self-produced by observer systems in the environment of other systems.*"[20] This claim means that any discussion of risk taking or risk making entails a reflective state of affairs and a decision about significance, a perfectly Weberian starting point.

Risk has been frequently coupled with "security." This coupling is polemically useful but analytically weak. If one opposes something and wants to discredit it, then it is smart to contrast risk with security (or safety). By so doing one implies that there exists a clear choice between a secure state of affairs and one that is not. Of course, the problem is that it is hard to see how anyone could choose the undesirable conditions rather than the desirable ones. If choosing security is a fool's paradise, another way forward is to make the primary distinction risk/danger instead of risk/security. By so doing one shifts the focus from a quest for security to an attention to possible future loss. In this mode one can make a link between a potential loss and a string of decisions that might lead to it: at that point one is speaking of risk, or, as Luhmann says, "the risk of decision." Once one begins to operate within the logic of risk and danger, the horizon of safety by no means disappears; rather, it remains unmarked in the linguistic sense. Within the pair of risk/danger one can emphasize either side: if one downplays the side of decision making, then "the possible loss is considered to have been caused externally; that is to say, it is attributed to the environment. In this case we speak of danger" (21). Those who mark risk downplay dangers; "whereas marking dangers allows the profits to be forgotten that could be earned if risky decisions are made" (24). A reflective observer sees that there can be no risk-free behavior. Deciding to act poses risks of loss in the future, but the observer notes that it is equally true that not acting carries with it its own consequences.

Luhmann draws two further consequences relevant here. He calls the first "the contingency schema." If one is concerned with the issue of future loss and of decision making, then we are faced with "two temporal contingencies, event and loss are firmly coupled as contingencies (not as facts!), this makes it possible for observers to differ in the way they see things. Temporal contingencies provoke social contingencies, and this plurality cannot be cancelled out by an ontological formula" (17). For Luhmann, accepting contingency means taking up a modern ethos toward the modern world.

Luhmann's second insight rejoins Canguilhem: "Modern risk-oriented society is a product not only of the perception of the consequences of technological achievement. Its seed is contained in the expansion of research possibilities and of knowledge itself" (28). The more science we do, the more knowledge we make, the more technological intervention becomes possible, the more choices are posed, the more risk there is, the more the imperative to act or not to act imposes itself. And that point must be the beginning of seeing what difference today makes with respect to yesterday: vigilance and intervention *même combat*.

Contemporary Formations

Although Habermas, Canguilhem, and Luhmann are helpful in different ways, none of them sufficiently problematizes the contemporary. Habermas is hypervigilant about dangers; his diagnostic of the present leads him to seek transcendental protection—the moral is untouched by the ethical—thereby deterring him from staying close to those changes, and consequently devoting himself to thinking about, or evaluating, them in their specificity and singularity, that is to say in their reality. Luhmann (as I argue in the "Observation" chapter) provides an epochal diagnosis of modernity as based on contingency, but by so doing he slips into a position of a first-order observer, a position that a second-order observer would have to qualify as contingent. Luhmann knows this, but even he is carried away into reifying modernity as risk society. Canguilhem acutely analyzes shifting scientific and technological changes but takes them up as fundamentally unproblematic; while such a position entails that he keep close to emerging practices of knowledge, it does not allow him to pay sufficient attention to the risk dimension that such practices open up. An anthropology of the contemporary thus faces the challenge of finding a means to remain close to diverse current practices producing knowledge, ethics, and politics, while adopting an attitude of discernment and adjacency in regard to them, thereby providing a space for a more precise and better formulation of contemporary problems and risks.

Conclusion

We learned from Darwin that humans are part of the animal kingdom. We are merely one species among a vast array of living beings, all subject to the great scheme of evolution and governed by natural selection. Freud called this insight one of the three great blows to humanity's narcissism. So here we are today, amidst a new set of claims and insights, attempting to sort out the scientific wheat from the scientific chaff. One touchstone for such sorting is to be attentive to anthropomorphic metaphors that pervade scientific prose.

Researchers at McGill Medical Center recently reported, in a *Science* article entitled "Nongenomic Transmission across Generations of Maternal Behavior and Stress Responses in the Rat," that variations in maternal care seem to influence how the young respond to stress—those that are given less care are more stressed.[21] This result is not that surprising. Of more interest is the article's claim to evidence of a neo-Lamarckian mode of transmission: the "transmission of such individual differences in maternal behavior from one generation of females to the next through behavior." This conclusion was arrived at through highly intrusive (if carefully controlled) intervention. Mother rats vary in the degree to which they care for (lick, groom, and nurse) the pups in their nest. When researchers placed pups from a "low-care" mom's litter into a "high-care" mom's nest, they observed that these pups were less fearful and became "more caring" than other offspring of "low-care" females. Simply said, more care in one generation yielded more care in the next generation.

The McGill researchers go hurtling down a slippery slope in search of molecules (they show that mRNA levels for certain hormones and binding activity of a hormone receptor vary among pups with "low-care" and "high-care" moms). They argue that since twin studies "suggest genetic inheritance" plays a role in personality, it would make sense to look for such genes in rats. Having established some correlations between rat behavior and the expression of a few genes in their brains, our researchers then conclude that their finding has implications for humans: "In humans, social, cultural, emotional and economic contexts influence the quality of the relationship between parent and child and can show continuity across generations. Our findings in rats may thus be relevant in understanding the importance of early intervention programs in humans." The circle is closed. The bow to socially useful science has been made.

The article contains some anthropocentric slips in its tight scientific prose that raise warning flags for an anthropologist. For example, "Individual differences in personality traits appear to be transmitted from parents to offspring. A critical question, however, concerns the mode of inheritance." Actually, the first critical question is the definition of an "individual" in the world of laboratory rats, and the second question is what could be meant by a rat's "personality"? "Personality" refers to "persons." Persons, from *persona* in Roman law, are moral figures. There are no such beings in the world of rats. Our researchers would do well to adopt a more precise vocabulary.

There is a double take-home message: (1) humanity's self-image has had a rough millennium (consequently bioscientists should learn to be attentive to their anthropomorphisms); (2) whatever your species, love and care for your offspring (support Head Start). Opening the door for an understanding of a "mechanism of a nongenomic mode of inheritance" might well show that genes have a range of variability in their expression, depending on the environment. The same genes express themselves differently in different settings. Genes, one should say, are part of a more complex picture that must include the genome, although that step is hardly the end of the story, only the end of a beginning.

It is easy to agree with one of Habermas's conclusions: "The new technologies make a public discourse on the right understanding of cultural forms of life in general an urgent matter. And philosophers no longer have any good reasons for leaving a dispute to biologists and engineers intoxicated by science fiction."[23] I agree. I would add, however, that anthropologists no longer have any good reason to leave such matters to sober philosophers devoted to an ascetic ideal of an undamaged life without risks, as the universal norm of our species morality. Let us return instead to the actual world of the contemporary with its messy ethical problems, its diverse forms of knowledge, its pedagogical and political challenges. Along with Michel Foucault, let me advocate a "patient labor giving form to our impatience for freedom." Such work may prove irritating and insufficient for some, but for others it is the path to a *Lebensführung worthy of the contemporary, that is to say, one attentive to emergent logoi* claiming to tell us who we really are, ones that need to be taken into account, appropriately, as one dimension, but only one dimension, of the risky practice of assembling a different figure of anthropos.

Thus, we are at the end of the beginning once again, and with Max Weber we must say: "The only question that remains is the sense in which science [*Wissenschaft*] gives 'no' answer, and whether or not science [*Wissenschaft*] might yet be of some use to the one who puts the question correctly."[22]

✴

ADJACENCY

Adjacent: in close proximity. May or may not imply
contact but always implies absence of anything of the
same kind in between.

One of the most telling incidents from my first field
work, in Morocco in 1968, concerned the relative
place of timing, situation, and telos in ethnographic
work. My memory (faulty as it may be) is that my advisor, Clifford Geertz, laid down a stern admonishment to Lawrence
Rosen, another University of Chicago graduate student, and
myself: we should not waste our time with peripheral matters,
however tempting they might appear, because something highly
distinctive and more important was passing from the scene. The
admonition was directed at Rosen's interest in the Jewish community of Morocco and mine in the French. As the second wing
of his "Islam Observed" project, Geertz's attention was focused
on the Islamic Moroccans, and he insisted we follow suit. Just
imagine, he said, if you were present in the Middle Ages and had
the opportunity of describing daily life in an important market
town. It is our obligation, he declared emphatically, to witness
and to record as much of what is taking place as we possibly can.

At the time, I thought this dicta was off base for a number of
simple reasons. First, I was not a partisan of "salvage" anthropology—the idea that the role of ethnography was to record the
"world on the wane" as it faded into oblivion. Second, then as

now my interests are as much anthropological as ethnographic; that is to say, the premise that description could not be easily separated from interpretation, and that the compelling reason to do ethnography in the first place had as much to do with broad theoretical questions about humanity as with the specifics of exotic customs. As Geertz himself would later wittily write, there was no point in going to Zanzibar in order to count cats. Third, alas, more substantively, the two cultures or social groups that were obviously in the process of waning were actually the Jews and the French. The majority Islamic Moroccans were certainly experiencing diverse pressures for change, but it was Geertz himself who had taught us about their immense tenacity and vitality.

I think this little incident has stayed with me over the decades because it embodies a distinctive double reversal, a kind of ethical and epistemological conundrum in which and through which many of us find ourselves perpetually seeking our way—and giving form to our selves and to our work. Superficially Geertz's admonition was after all self-deflating—if salvage was the key diacritic, then Rosen and I and Geertz should all have been spending our time in a kind of Fredric Wiseman attempt to record everything, obviously a hopeless task. However, on a different plane, that of scientific humility, Geertz was on to something important. One of the key messages of Geertz's written work (and perhaps the core of this dictum can be taken as an ethical and epistemological aspect of all scientific work) is that one must strive to become, in one form or another, what Donna Haraway has called a "modest witness." That which one is trying to understand—even if, or especially if, it includes the self— must be made into an object of study. And, as any minimally coherent philosophical or social scientific understanding of *Wissenschaft* holds, that means it must be constructed. Witnesses witness things (be they saint's festivals or yeast reactions to salt) they have come to believe (for disciplinary, autobiographical, or more broadly ethical or political reasons) are significant. Modesty implies, at a minimum, that the things, the world, events, are what count most. But they count scientifically of course, and here there is a twist back on the vocational double helix, only to the degree that these things have been conceptualized, tested, and interpreted. Or at least are in the process of being conceptualized, tested and interpreted. But, as Weber hammered home a century ago, to be conceptualized, tested and interpreted, things need to be identified as significant. And that nominalist task does not arise spontaneously from the things themselves.[1] Or, as Geertz put it once, anthropologists study villages, good anthropologists study processes in villages. Choosing those processes is not mere witnessing but is itself an act of interpretation, or diagnosis.

Timing

George Marcus astutely raises the issue of time, or better timing, in ethnographic research and writing in an article entitled "On the Unbearable Slowness of Being an Anthropologist Now: Notes on a Contemporary Anxiety in the Making of Anthropology." Although Marcus is concerned with the profession of anthropology, and the production and dissemination of ethnographic texts, the topic of time pressures certainly arises in the biosciences as well. Marcus's article provides an excellent starting point for further questioning, further inquiry, and consequent reformulation of questions.

Marcus opens his article with a quote from an essay by Pierre Bourdieu entitled "The Scholastic Point of View":

> In contradistinction to Plato's lawyer, or Cicourel's physician, we have all the time in the world, all our time, and this freedom from urgency, from necessity—which often takes the

form of economic necessity, due to the convertibility of time into money—is made possible by an ensemble of social and economic conditions, by the existence of these supplies of free time that accumulated economic resources represent.[2]

Few, if any, molecular biologists or active anthropologists would ever imagine today that they had all the time in the world to do their work, to produce results, and to have them published. In the life sciences, the ferocious, ceaseless, and ever more accelerated competition for priority makes this view of the leisurely pursuit of truth strictly unimaginable. Normatively, however, Bourdieu's claim that scientific truths are timeless has its own plausibility. Who discovered, published, and patented the sequence of the BRCA1 gene matters only to the individual scientists (and their universities and companies). The discovery itself remains without historicity, as least for those who hold a realist view of scientific truth. A mutation is a mutation is a mutation. The traditional work of anthropologists fell, in a different manner, under that normativity of timelessness, as long as anthropology could maintain that the object of study (whether culture or society) was out of history or at least operating on a radically different temporality from that of the anthropologist in her modernity. A kinship system is a kinship system is a kinship system. Given this self-understanding, "anthropology could confidently insist on standards of research performance that valued deliberation, patience, and a stable scene and subject of study."[3] Such a position has not disappeared, but it is under renewed strain today.

Situating: Tolerance and Benevolence

For many anthropologists working on the contemporary world, there is what Marcus dryly calls "a hyper-desire to be relevant.

Under the pressure of cultural studies there emerged a particular figure of the academic scholar, the public intellectual. [and] a rhetoric of inquiry that emphasized relevance and the activist voice" (14). Here the anthropology of the contemporary "became driven by the same issues that defined NGOs, social movements, journalism, and left-liberal commentaries on the unfolding of distinctive events in the United States and elsewhere, in a world that was conceived to be globalizing." This drive and this politics run into a specific set of contemporary obstacles. Cultural studies has produced a vast corpus of critical writing that puts the legitimacy, not to mention the very existence, of the public sphere into question. To then turn around, as Marcus observes, and seek to be political by writing op-ed pieces or becoming advisors to policy makers, or shaping foundation programs, demonstrates a lack of a consistency of vision, although it is certainly a mode of accumulation of capital both symbolic and material. At the beginning of the twenty-first century, the performance of confidently speaking truth to power, of proudly bearing the privileged insights of anthropology to the wider world, of moralistically upping the anthropologist, appears disquietingly quaint. The bad news (or in some cases almost any news) has not yet arrived from the field and to the discipline. That by no means implies that anthropological work cannot reach broader audiences, but how to create those audiences, or invent forms to influence, instruct, or outrage them, is another matter.

Although my own work on the milieu of biotechnology is certainly contemporary, qua anthropologist or philosopher, I have been driven by a desire neither to have an activist voice per se nor to join the world of NGOs and op-ed pieces (although as a citizen I certainly share the goals and effects of some of the causes these organizations champion). When confronted (by others or by myself) with the question of why I am doing this work, I often say "because it interests me." As I realize each time

I utter this phrase (to myself or to others), that answer is both a conversation stopper and a provocation. It is a conversation stopper because what is there to say in response? For working scientists this kind of claim seems to be self-evident. It is a equally a provocation, however, because today in the Anglophone academy there always seems to be a demand for a surplus to curiosity, whether it be ethical, political, or commercial. Thus the response is never quite satisfying either to those I am interviewing or to myself and the demons that haunt me.

Hence as I was beginning my work with Roger Brent, the director of the Molecular Sciences Institute in Berkeley, while sitting in a small Berkeley café eating a wonderful Persian-Californian fusion sandwich on a warm September afternoon in 2002, feeling perfectly ethical because even though I had not yet received approval from the Berkeley Committee for the Protection of Human Subjects (more below), I had been informed that it was officially permitted to talk to Human Subjects outside of the workplace, I told Roger (in response to his query about what I hoped to achieve by working with him and his lab) that I thought it was an important thing in a democracy that there were citizens who took the time to inform themselves in some detail about what genomics actually was, so that these informed people would be able to contribute to a more enlightened public discussion. Just as he generously accepted my claim to curiosity as sufficient, he enthusiastically acquiesced to this supplement, saying he now understood better what I am trying to do and was happy to contribute to this aspect of the project as well.

Roger was raised in the Deep South and has strong political views about the need for supporting a politics of equality and justice in America, views that I share. He also works with the government on issues related to defense against biological attack because he feels strongly that the United States is "hideously vulnerable" to bioterrorism. He feels it is urgent and imperative to change that vulnerability.

Roger (he might be surprised to know) is a "specific intellectual." The term was coined by Foucault as a contrast term to the figure of the "universal intellectual."[4] The universal intellectual was the Man of Letters who spoke in the name of the Universal. Today in the United States Noam Chomsky does his best to perform the role of the universal intellectual. As long as the figure is recognized, it does not have to be explained why a specialist on transformational grammar (funded by the navy and working at MIT) should be given special credence when he makes pronouncements on American foreign policy. He is not an expert in that area in the technical sense, although he is certainly well informed, if highly partial; rather, Chomsky is a voice of Justice and Reason. In contrast, Foucault argued, the specific intellectual spoke from within a particular technical formation in which he or she was a qualified and credentialed participant. Brent can talk about bioterrorism because he is an expert on protein-protein interaction (his lab works on them) and nucleic acid detection methods (he edits a standard manual). Consequently, although bioterrorism is not precisely Brent's area of expertise, it is close enough that he can produce informed statements about the subject that carry authority—authority within the community of researchers struggling with detection and antidote problems, authority within an adjacent group of government policymakers whose charge is to develop such procedures, and authority in a wider sphere should he choose to exercise it and prove capable of finding a means of doing so (forums, journalism, etc.).

Where am I situated within this political space? Neither as a universal intellectual nor as a specific intellectual. I am adjacent to both. "Adjacent: in close proximity. May or may not imply contact but always implies absence of anything of the same kind in between." Neither the overdrive of the universal intellectual nor the authoritative precision of the specific. Rather: a space of problems. Of questions. Of being behind or ahead. Belated or anticipatory. Out of synch. Too fast or too slow. Reluctant. Audacious. Annoying.

Anthropologists, Marcus observes, are exposed to a politics of knowledge today of a wildly diverse sort. This twin point of my being situated as an anthropologist and the politics of knowledge as a complex site where interconnections cannot be assumed was brought to the fore in an exchange that took place at the Molecular Sciences Institute. The institute has a weekly meeting each Friday at one. The meeting takes place in Berkeley, and many of the eight to ten people present in the lab at one time assemble in the meeting room, where there is an audio conferencing hookup with one of their chief collaborators at MIT, and less frequently at Cal Tech. One Friday while waiting for the group to assemble, and still in the process of finding my feet with these people, I make some kind of small comment to one of the scientists.

I tell them that I am in the process of filing a Human Subjects Application to protect them against my possible violation of their rights. I tell them that I find this requirement onerous and, in the way it is shaped, rather stupid. I tell them that when I answered the question about how this research will benefit humanity I wrote a few sentences quoting and then paraphrasing the essay of Immanuel Kant on "What Is Enlightenment?" in which Kant proposes that the task of enlightenment is simultaneously to "dare to know" and to do so in a manner in which one strives for an independent use of one's reason. The latter use of one's reason, when it is unfettered from state or other authorities, however tolerant and beneficial they may be, constitutes a mature use of reason. The mature use of reason will respect the current laws of a country as the price of this unfettered practice of free thought and reflection. The Human Subjects Protocol in this setting seems to me—and to many others—the kind of tutelage that is so common in contemporary America (and elsewhere where bureaucracies administer funds for those seeking natural or human scientific truths through systematic inquiry); that is to say, filling in papers to feed a bureaucracy that operates on universal principles that fail to distinguish the simple differences between things. Thus the process does not begin by noting the difference between administering a therapeutic (or hopefully therapeutic) drug to a patient and interviewing a CEO of one of the most powerful companies in the world. Both processes begin in the same manner; each is a Human Subject whose rights need to be protected through a small ritual of informed consent. Stage 1 and 2 clinical trials for ethics.

There is no discernable reaction to my little speech. People are getting their lunch ready or making sure the projector works or finding the video on the Web that they are going to project during the meeting.

As things are still in flux I make the second point. There is another clause in the protocol for studies involving subjects of race and ethnicity. I say that I wrote that anthropologists had rejected this language for more than fifty years. That "race" had no scientific meaning when it came to human beings, and that if one had to use the term at all, there would probably be a large number of populations and in any case not three. I further added that when asked on forms to identify myself I often put down "pink."[5] One reason is that I simply cannot bring myself to check the box "Caucasian." If anyone cares, and they usually do not, I say that the peoples from the Caucasus slaughtered my ancestors in various pogroms and therefore I could not identify with them. I have rarely if ever gotten a reaction to this declaration. This void is no doubt in part due to the fact that people are trained to "respect" others—racial identifications in the United States after all are "self-reported," and they are freighted, highly charged. So why ask for trouble?

One scientist perks up at this point and says that of course there are races, anyone can see that. I say that race is no longer used as a scientific concept for Homo Sapiens. He looks at me blankly. He repeats that race is a perfectly good category; that the phenotype must indicate something genetic. I find myself at a loss. I have basically only arguments from authority available to me—"no one in anthropology has said anything like that in fifty years," "Lewontin has shown that there is as much variation within groups as between them." These claims carry no weight at all with my interlocutor. No one else intervenes in this discussion. I expect Roger to say something but he does not. Perhaps there is some larger background to this that I am unaware of, or he finds the discussion of no interest, or he feels it is not his role to intervene. Then the meeting starts.

What is one to make of this exchange? First, that being a traditional "fly on the wall" observer who did not interact with those he was studying would certainly not have gotten me into this exchange. That would have been a loss. Second, the small talk and banter that I thought I was engaged in, absolutely taken for granted in the circles I generally move in, here was taken as a strange speech act. It was not responded to in scientific terms but utterly and simply in terms of the person's common sense. Hence and furthermore, the idea that one always has a critical meta-observational sense of what one says is totally lacking here. He made no apparent effort—or so it seems to me—to connect the hypersophisticated science the institute was doing and his own views of things. "Of course black people are different."

The excellent book by Jennifer Reardon, *Race to the Finish*, on the launch and failure of the Human Genome Diversity Project demonstrates this point on a bigger canvas.[6] This project, spearheaded by the population geneticist Luca Cavalli-Sforza at Stanford but joined by highly placed and frequently consulted lawyer-ethicists like Henry Greely at Stanford, proposed in the light of the project to map the human genome that another project be set in motion that would record the human diversity of the species before it disappeared. The fact that there are two doctoral theses concerned with the project indicates the complexity and interest of the topic. To make a long story short, the project never succeeded in getting under way. It was challenged on biological grounds that its conceptions of isolated populations would not bear much scrutiny, and it was challenged on ethical grounds that it had not taken the Human Subjects factors sufficiently into account. There was a long period of debate and contestation on these two fronts, and many changes were made. But the project was also questioned on political grounds: who had the right to represent the peoples of the world? What possible benefit there would be to these people? Who should own the patents and make the profits presumed to be the motivation for the project behind its performance of scientific curiosity and innocence?

It was the performance of innocence of such questions (however one decided to answer them) that caught me off guard at the Molecular Sciences Institute. "These things are self-evident," "why are you being stupid," "it goes without saying," "I don't see an issue here." Parallel reactions (although increasingly more cautious ones) took place within the diversity project, leading to a "model protocol" and a set of changes within the sampling techniques both as to how the sampling was to be carried out in practical terms and how the samples were to be defined. But the politics was never solved, and the federal government backed off. The Human Genome Diversity Project does not exist.

No one at the lab reacted. The conclusion I drew from this incident was that it required a form of pedagogical response. Consequently, as Roger Brent and I are going to teach a course on genomics and citizenship at Berkeley, we must include a section on race. Lecturing the scientists at the lab before their meeting, however, seemed inappropriate, especially before I was fully certified as ethical.

Imagine my surprise several months later during preliminary discussions in my department about hiring two junior anthropologists. The first step was to establish a preliminary long list of preferred candidates. However, colleagues committed to diversity combed through the entire list of applicants to make sure we had not ignored qualified "underrepresented minorities," as the phrase goes. Several candidates were identified by colleagues as possibly being "minority." This tentative identification was made on the content of their research. Although no one would dare directly ask the potential candidate if he or she fit the category, as that would have been unethical and unseemly, informal meetings with them were arranged. And as they all turned out to be "white," their candidacy was terminated.[7]

Telos: A Zone of Discomfort

The issue of *telos* is an especially vexed one. There are zones of representation that pre-exist and surpass whatever an anthropologist does, especially the anthropologist driven by a desire to be relevant in her interventions. As Marcus observes, "Rarely does an anthropologist take up a topic of interest that has not already been more prominently and more promptly treated by other media—prestige and resource rich journalism being only the most common example" (16). Marcus is certainly correct that there is a vein of rich journalism that succeeds in covering fields like biotechnology, venture capitalism, humanitarian aid, bioweapons, global finance, sex trade, and like topics in a timely and intelligent fashion. One should add immediately that there is a great deal of journalism that is timely but highly formulaic. One only has to look at the books written about the Human Genome Mapping Project to see what a journalistic formula looks like. There are things to learn from these books, especially the techniques used to be timely. But equally there is much to ponder about how an anthropology of the actual, which seeks to be more timely than traditional anthropology in both its subject matter and its forms of presentation, would differ from journalism.

The best of the scientific journalists (and I assume this applies in other specialties in a parallel fashion) have access to almost anyone they seek to speak to (when the *New York Times* calls, people answer). The journalist, however, usually wants to speak about a specific subject and for a specific amount of time. And to specific leaders who, not by accident, are habituated to producing succinct summaries. The journalist has deadlines and a story to tell. The story almost always must conform to a set of genre prescriptions, learned through practice and actively enforced by editors. Stories must be "lively," have "a plot," be "clear," not be too "technical," "make its points," be "interesting," etc. Like any form that has been in use for a while, its strengths are also its weaknesses. There is no point in reading all the journalistic books about the genome because they are more or less the same. One may be "livelier" than the next, another "more informed," another "better told," but they are telling the same story because that story is what has been sold to the publisher, and only subsequently to the public. Furthermore, the story line had been previously crafted in the daily, weekly, or monthly columns of the journalist already frequently in ongoing contact with the scientists who are being interviewed. Nikolas Wade has talked to Craig Venter or Francis Collins before. They can be quick with each other. And, in a rather more masked fashion, with us.

Not only must the journalistic story not be too technical scientifically, apparently it is even more imperative that no concepts from other academic disciplines be mentioned explicitly. There is a marked vexation among journalists, which is echoed among many of the scientists with whom I have worked, whenever social science or philosophic terms are introduced. Thus, to give one recent example, a highly intelligent professional journalist acquaintance was explaining to me the need to be crystal clear how the different opinions of various actors in the biotechnology industry were "subjective." I remarked in passing that I agreed with the need to contextualize opinion. She looked at me with mild amazement, tinged with raised-eyebrows vigilance, and asked what the word meant. To her this term was social scientific jargon and consequently unacceptable to those writing clearly. That is to say, a term that has attained the status of a commonplace within the social sciences, "contextualization," is confidently held to be unmentionable elsewhere. "No Concepts Please—we are reaching the public." Or: "Fixed Genres and Clear English Prose Only—the public has attention deficit disorder." In sum, just as I am adjacent to the scientists I am working with, so, too I find myself adjacent to my journalist friends.

One encounters the dilemma of form and audience in other ways. Those of us working in the anthropology of science (whether genomic or environmental or others) find that we must make a choice as to whether or not we want our scientist friends and collaborators to read and comment on our work. "These natives," Marcus writes, "do not necessarily share the temporality and modes of writing of anthropology" (13). Although this claim is certainly true, there are a number of other aspects contributing to reception that are worth noting. One factor contributing to the willingness of scientists to cooperate with an anthropologist is a dissatisfaction with journalism. Irritation at the perceived partisanship or sensationalism or analytic thinness in the most prestigious and powerful journals, that is, *Science* and *Nature*, is a frequent refrain. Scientific journalism, for example, in the *New York Times*, might direct a molecular biologist to an article she hadn't noticed, but the *Times* article is never sufficiently technical to be a substitute for the original. Hence there exists a space of dissatisfaction of unfulfilled need adjacent to journalism and scientific journals. I think this is one reason many scientists read science fiction (and related fiction). In this writing there is an imaginative reformulation that provides a space of reflection, of objectivation or, shall we say, "contextualization." Hence neither journalism nor science fiction provides untimely and disquieting forms. And that is just fine for most people. These forms are, or can be, entertaining and instructive. In any case they are for "after hours"—a bit like the "ethics" that arrives after the scientific work on the genome has already been done. Such work would be good for the soul, if only we had one.

I am convinced by my fieldwork experience that there exists a virtual space of adjacency for other genres, other forms. It is a space of objectivity. One the one hand, it is a space of objectivity in the sense of disinterestedness: the anthropologist has neither the same interconnections, nor the same stakes, nor the same pressures that the journalists for *Science* or *Nature* do. The anthropologist is not trained in the world of molecular biology and is not writing within the strictures of its editorial expectations and constraints. On the other hand, there is a zone of adjacency in which a kind of objectivity can be made to function simply so as to pique the native's curiosity. That space of objectivity is one in which different constructions of the object are highlighted. Thus, some scientists will appreciate a certain conceptual distance from themselves, an unfamiliar sensibility in their midst, a foreign technicity about their work, echoes of a different conversation in which they figure. Here, contextualizations, oblique discussions, and meandering beyond the plotted story line may indeed be welcomed. In sum, the narrative style and content the anthropologist provides, if it has established its own authority, its credibility, provides a perspective rarely encountered in the hyperoccupied lives of big science. This perspective provides something new for the curious researcher; that something new might be called the truth-function of an untimely anthropology.

Finally, I believe that it is not a sociological accident that some of these scientists are willing to give of their time to exotic visitors. Rather, there is an unanticipated convergence of perspectives and challenges between certain anthropologists and certain scientists. I think it is accurate to say that these scientists are specialists in keeping their ears open. Marcus puts a parallel insight this way:

> There is a set of events that are localized but of global significance. The task is to find a way to bring them into analytic relationship with each other. These relations are sometimes obvious and sometimes take sustained fieldwork to identify. In fact, one of the skills and challenges facing the actors themselves is to identify trends, connections, emergent fields, possible shifts, etc. (12)

In previous work I referred to those who undertake this work as "technicians of general ideas."[8] "Understanding life," "curing disease," are general ideas. One segment of society is dedicated to approaching them through the deployment of ever greater, more sophisticated, expensive, and coordinated techno-science. Those doing this work are technicians and scientists. Those directing them might well be technicians of general ideas. Technicians of general ideas make good informants.

Untimely Work

The work of *Bildung* might seem to be individual. However, the examples discussed previously should indicate that this is not the case. First, even when there is work on the self it entails work that involves a doubling, an act of making oneself into an object upon which work can be performed. Thus, studious work on the self, taken up as truth seeker, is relational on multiple planes. Second, there is a moment of pedagogy. This moment can occur at different times. It might be the impulse to instruct in a limited and technical sense—"by contextualization historians mean," "anthropologists don't use the term race anymore." Or, it might be later in a formal site of instruction like the classroom or lec-

ture hall. Third, the practice of the kind of *Bildung* I am proposing is situated adjacent to other ethically practices like science or
journalism that can themselves take a vocational form (*Berufsar-
beit*). Thus anthropological inquiry is not primarily concerned
with undertaking direct dialogue, or producing conditions of
nondistorted communication—"let's talk this through," "let's see
if we can't agree." Work between vocations is not the same thing
as work among peers or among citizens. Its goal is not convincing the other of anything, if by convincing one means sustained
argumentation. Anthropological inquiry is based first and foremost on listening, observing, hearing, seeing, querying, sensing,
reflecting, pondering, wondering, and writing at various times
during, before, and after performing these other actions. Its goal
is identifying, understanding, and formulating something actual
neither by directly identifying with it nor by making it exotic.
Rather, it seeks to articulate a mode of adjacency. Such work may
be lonely—after all, who else wants to be untimely and adjacent—but it can never be done alone.

Today, resolute and ardent untimeliness is an important practice to foster. This admonition is not a plea for Bourdieu's
scholastic point of view as it does not seek to contribute to a
timeless theory. Although one must acknowledge that, for reasons that are almost entirely unexamined, industrial societies
have indeed provided the resources necessary for some to conduct a leisured, if not leisurely, exploration of things. Given this
space, and for as long as it lasts, we should be hard at work thinking, writing, inquiring. It follows that a central question before
us is: what form should this writing, thinking, and inquiring
take? And what norms should govern it? And to what telos does
it strive?

Thus, this anthropological practice is characterized by what
might be called a mode of virtual untimeliness. Let me explain.
The difference between a mode of potentiality and what Deleuze
has called a mode of virtuality consists in the fact that potential-

49

ity actualizes a state, a quality, or a form that is already inherent or resident in the being, thing, or process under consideration.[9] The mode of virtuality does not directly partake of this metaphysical world. It operates adjacent to it, moving along side potentialities and actualities so that these can be taken up and refracted in another form. In another mode. That is to say, the virtual as opposed to the potential is a mode replete with real things and processes but redirected, removed from their habitual courses. Traditionally, my diagnosis and prescription is for those working within a space of anthropological *Bildung* not to look within but to be constantly working out, so as to create better forms for the self, for others, and for things.

Thus, the problem with Geertz's admonition was that it assumed one knew already what was actual and what was passing away. Of course his was an informed assumption that corresponded well to what he considered to be significant. However, relevance, one might say, is a relative thing. Thus, if one is committed to untimely anthropological work then being a bit late may well be timely; and being ahead of things, or slightly beside the point, is worth our while.

✳

OBSERVATION

The recent past has seen a number of relatively new forms of anthropological practice emerging; others most certainly will be invented in the near future. Among the current approaches is one that I have been experimenting with, one that privileges extensive interviewing with a distinctive group of actors, within a restricted field setting. This approach is consequently faced with a challenge of what form to give this material. Such a site-restricted, directed interview-oriented form of inquiry can be contrasted to the more traditional ethnographic practice of broad-ranging observation that orients itself to multiple contexts and actors, aiming at a comprehensive understanding of a group's social relations, cultural symbols, psychological patterns, and the like. In this standard form, the ethnographer is physically present but in spite of all its prescriptions to participate would be just as happy not to do so. Should it ever prove to be possible to occupy the proverbial position of "fly on the wall," then the job of observing, documenting, and interpreting multiple situations, ongoing interactions, and actor networks without disturbing them could satisfy the panoptic desire embedded in that mode of work. This desire, of course, would have to question whether it shared the goals of Foucault's Panopticism in that the architects of the latter sought to develop and perfect observational technology aimed at producing mute, disciplined, and productive bodies. The standard participant observation ethnography wants, above all, not to change anything the natives are busy doing, thinking, and feeling. A third position is that of writing a genealogy of the Panopticon (or other arts and techniques) with the goal neither to discipline nor to oversee but to render things visible and vulnerable. My current experimentation with form and mode requires me to bypass all three of the above alternatives.

From its inception, the traditional ethnographic approach has run into a core set of limitations, all connected to its initial privileging of the subject/object distinction. One reaction to this dilemma has been to privilege a norm of objectivity—social facts are things—and to introduce a therapeutics of the observer as a means of overcoming subjective bias. The use of a range of technologies to purify the subject has been prominent in American anthropology at least since Margaret Mead and her generation's pervasive interest in psychoanalysis as a method to reveal the deepest secrets of a culture as well as the projections of the anthropologist's own culture onto the object of study.[1] In that form of analysis, subjectifying techniques became a type of hygienics used to identify symptomatic patterns and to objectify them so as to make them available, eventually, for better scientific observation. This goal is one shared by those who counseled psychotherapy for fledgling anthropologists so that they could ablate themselves from their own cultural prejudices, or by those more sophisticated psychoanalytic approaches that brought transference and countertransference into account with the goal of overcoming the analytic noise in the observational system. Later, in the last several decades of the twentieth century, strategies for coping with the subject/object distinction shifted: subjectifying practices moved from being a site of preliminary purification to a sui generis object of inquiry. Confessional discourses and deployed voices gained prominence within certain sectors of American anthropology (although they were never dominant). Although a salutary counterweight to some of the epistemologically exhausted forms of objectivism (which had become increasingly obsessed with method), this subjectifying countermove has itself proved to me more reactive than creative of new modes of inquiry or forms of writing. There is a dream of transparency at work; if there were a way for the informant to speak into the tape recorder (or point the camera lens) without the anthropologist saying anything, then the distinction would be fully operationalized. As graduate students have been gravely reminded for generations, the point of our profession is not "you," it is the "other." Again, if only one could disappear entirely and let the other speak, the science will have matured. Thus, this form of participant observation starts with the distinction that culture has a unity, the encultured or socialized individual has a self, one infused with the culture; the anthropologist is herself a bearer of a self and a culture that only adequate scientific treatment can induce to recede asymptotically. Then, and only then, the immediacy of the other, appropriated and appreciated, would be available. The moral imperative driving these distinctions was a perfectly admirable attempt to valorize cultural difference.

Once it is seen that ethnographic practice could proceed from other distinctions, however, the previous form loses, at a minimum, if not its authority, at least its self-evidence. The turn to explore other possibilities was ardently resisted within the discipline mainly because the previous form had been so heavily invested with moral assumptions and affects that were held to cohere in an unbreakable manner with scientific principles. Sundering these connections, or making them available for questioning, proved painful for many, but in reality it in no way foreclosed the practice of anthropology. Quite the contrary, problematizing previously taken-for-granted apparatuses makes it clear that other modes and forms are possible and at least potentially feasible. For them to be actualized, however, requires not only rethinking but equally a corrosion of the power relations embedded in the *habitus* of a generation. Such change takes time.

What if we did not begin with the distinction of subject and object and its secondary assumption that it is the culture that is enunciated through speaking subjects? What if we did not begin with the distinction between a whole to be captured and an inquiring subject to be rendered transparent? What if we did not begin with the assumption that our task was to write culture? And what if the search for another form of anthropological inquiry proceeded from a different set of distinctions? What then would observation consist in? And what operations would assist that new form of observation?

Bildung

Here the term *Bildung* is at least partially appropriate. In his essay "On the Anthropological and Semantic Structure of *Bildung*," Reinhart Koselleck eruditely unpacks the conceptual history of a term that had an influential past but has fallen into a state of disuse and discredit today.[2] While not entirely archaic, the term has lost most of its older cultural punch; it has become unmoored from the semantic and institutional field in which it arose and which, to a degree, it helped to shape. As its original docking conditions are no longer actual, the term is, as it were, adrift, gently bobbing up and down in the calm backwaters of the world's conceptual reservoir. The methodology of *Begriffsgeschichte* is designed to free concepts from their previous social and cultural embeddedness by showing the historicity of that embeddedness and hence its contingency. Thus, the first step in a critical process of reappropriation of this or any other concept is to contextualize the concept's emergence and its associations.

Koselleck and his team systematically pared away associations that had accreted around the concept but, they argue convinc-

54

ingly, had not been essential to it. Thus, one of the reasons that *Bildung* has fallen into disuse is that the term had been laden with the legacy of Goethe's Romantic heroes struggling with the fate of their soul amidst a philistine cultural world of the rising bourgeoisie; or, later, with Thomas Mann's depiction of the educated commercial classes of a bygone era, coming to terms with the pathos of their class's world historical decline. Thus the term is linked to stylizations and technologies of former modes of self-formation, as well as their associated social locations: first the refined court aristocracy and then the bourgeoisie's civic and religious seriousness with its fraught relationship to capitalism and imperialism. Koselleck and his team demonstrate the contingency of what had previously been assumed to be the inherent links of *Bildung* with bourgeois culture by showing that the concept had preceded its bourgeois articulation, and outlasted it as well, albeit in a marginal form. Furthermore, even during the time of bourgeois ascendancy, *Bildung* had been made to function critically at the individual, cultural, and political levels.

Thus, is it possible to reinterpret *Bildung*, as Foucault did with "Enlightenment," as a term whose referent and concept turn on a form of ethos rather than on an epochal designation? Like Enlightenment, one source of the term's prominence is precisely its malleable deployment in diverse social and political sites. *Bildung* could not exist without a social structural setting, but it is not reducible to that setting. Koselleck writes, "*Bildung* is a peculiar, self-inducing pattern of behavior and form of knowledge that remains reliant on economic presuppositions and political conditions in order to flourish; but this does not mean that *Bildung* can be causally and sufficiently derived from these conditions."[3] Unlike Enlightenment, *Bildung* has no exact equivalent in French or English.[4] Although the standard English translation of *Bildung* is "character," Koselleck suggests that "Self-formation, a word coined by the Earl of Shaftesbury in the eighteenth century that influenced the German concept of *Bildung*, is preferable" (173). However, the current fascination with the self and subjectivity in the Anglophone world makes this translation an easily misleading one. As Koselleck puts it, "*Bildung* forms: it is itself a genuine historical factor" (173). Specifically, *Bildung* can be distinguished semantically from either formal education (*Ausbildung*) and or cultivated imagination (*Einbildung*).[5] So the concept itself can be equated neither with an institution nor with a product possessed by those who take themselves for educated. Having a Ph.D., even in the humanities, does not bestow *Bildung*, nor is it the kind of thing that buying even the most expensive liberal arts education or self-improvement trainers can ensure.

In passing Koselleck observes a distinction that historically had marked a difference between *Bildung* and Enlightenment:

> While Enlightenment appealed to reason, by which humans should allow themselves to be guided, and to nature, knowledge of which would provide permanent rules and laws for all spheres of experience, and while of both of these tasks simultaneously established social, economic, political, and collective historical goals, *Bildung* challenged a large multitude of human possibilities. (180)

Consequently, *Bildung* entailed more than the cultivation of reason, although it certainly could—and as concerns my project must—include the problematization of reason as well. Among the challenges relevant to *anthropos* today is how to take up reason as a constitutive element of a form of life when its guidelines continue to command inclusion but are understood to be both contingent and malleable. Also, how to take up nature as a constitutive element of a form of life when its rules and laws can be modified through the use of reason. Said another way: What form of *Bildung* is appropriate to a contemporary conduct of life (Weber's *Lebensführung*)? Is there a form of *Bildung* appropriate to the anthropology of the contemporary?

Some of the conditions that such a form would have to meet are set out in a perspicacious collection of Niklas Luhmann's essays entitled *Observations on Modernity*. Among the pertinent topics is the place of the future in modernity.[6] For Luhmann, a key question today is how the future appears: What is its modality? And given that modality, what form should observation take? Luhmann's answers are: (1) The future appears as a contingent set of possibilities about which decisions are demanded; decisions are demanded because the future appears as something about which we must do something. (2) The appropriate form of analysis consists in observing observers observing. What does this mean?

Observing the Future

In an essay entitled "Describing the Future," Luhmann addresses the issue of what form the future is being given today as well as what forms predictions about it take, in a society that understands itself to be ever-accelerating.[7] Although our times abound in futurologists, prophets, and prognosticators, it is hard, Luhmann sarcastically observes, to take them seriously as we actually have very little sense of what a future not yet visible in the present would look like in any detail. Two confirmatory examples are, first, the world-historical failure of the experts to predict how the Soviet empire would end (although a multitude of volumes now show how it was inevitable); and second, even more pertinently, the fact that for a couple of years Bill Gates missed the import of the Internet. Luhmann argues that posing the question of the future in terms of form rather than content will produce sociologically more powerful insights.[8] He argues that the only genre of answer to this question that should be taken seriously is one that turns on the future appearing as contingent, one that (for that very reason) compels incessant decisions.

Of course, descriptions of the future are hardly an invention of modern times. Luhmann presents a standard history of ideas perspective that holds that until far into the eighteenth century, social life was experienced within a cosmos of essences that guaranteed the constancy of forms of being as well as their constituent elements. The "*harmonia mundi*" was beyond question. Within such a frame, what was at issue was not the appearance of any startling new things, but, concern over what would happen. Variation took place on the level of events. Fortune-telling as well as expert prognostication turned on specification and hope and fear. Following various eighteenth-century trends, and becoming embodied in a form around the time of the French Revolution, there appeared a newly conceived trust in the future: "Perfection was followed by perfectibility."[9] That which was could be improved. New things could come into being and new types of things could happen. Such perfectibility and its associated optimism are embodied in the diverse notions of progress and utility that proliferated throughout the late Enlightenment and permeated the rationality of modernity.[10] What Luhmann refers to as "Humankind" moved beyond a self-understanding that assumed a pregiven form of perfection into uncharted spaces with a great deal more latitude for individuals to make the world and themselves as well as for a population that improves itself by selection on an individual level. Although Luhmann does not mention him, this political rationality that links individuals to populations in a field of living beings is Foucault's biopower. "All in all," Luhmann observes, "we have the impression that around 1800 the impossibility of describing the new structures of modern society would be compensated for with projections of the future."[11] Both in the technological and in the humanistic spheres, society described itself in the projection of its future. This moment is of course also the moment in which a new understanding of the past, as history, was being articulated throughout the European elite, as Reinhart Koselleck has documented.[12] To the challenge of how finitude should be incorporated, the answer was to engage in the infinite task of seeking norms and forms adequate to it.

In our time, as never before, the continuity from past to future is broken. However, the one thing we do know is that much of what will be true in future presents will depend on current decisions. Decide now! To further complicate the picture, we do not have anyone who really *can* decide. It so happens that we live at a time in which the social authority of experts has been undermined by their oft-proven inability either to forecast the future or to make it happen as envisioned. Dryly and without pathos or nostalgia, Luhmann calls that which has taken the place of authority "the politics of understanding." Understandings are negotiated provisos that can be relied upon for a given time. Such understandings do not imply consensus, nor do they represent reasonable or even correct solutions to problems. What they do do is attempt to fix reference points. Reference points are those things that are removed from the argument for further controversies in which coalitions and oppositions can form anew. Understandings have one big advantage over the claims of authority: they cannot be discredited but can only be constantly renegotiated. Finally, their value does not increase but only decreases with age.

Luhmann's point helps to explain why we continue to turn to experts whose predictions of twenty years ago now look ridiculous: they may have been wrong, but at least they are helpful in framing a discussion.[13] Of course, following the media whirlwind, everyone agrees that cloning is vitally important—the president wants a position soon—hurry, let's have a weighty discussion about its future impact, round up the usual value spokespeople, and be sure a broad spectrum of views is represented. Express concern! Issue a report!

It follows that a key diacritic of contemporary modernity lies in the form taken by the temporality of the future. For us, the present refers to a future that only exists as what is probable or improbable. Said another way, the form of the future is the form of probability that directs a two-sided observation as something more or less probable or more or less improbable, with a distribution of these modalities across everything that is possible. The present can calculate a future that can always turn out otherwise. The present can in this way always assure itself that it calculated correctly, even if things turn out differently. Such a situation does not rule out prognoses. In fact, it incessantly demands it, but its only worth lies in the quickness with which it can be corrected and/or more commonly simply forgotten. There exists, therefore, only a "provisional" foresight, whose function is found in the form it provides for a quick adjustment to a reality that comes to be other than what was (then) expected.

It is in such a situation that one finds the modern type of expert, that is, someone who, when asked questions he cannot answer, responds—but in a mode that can eventually be led back to a mode of respectable uncertainty. With a little distance, experts and counterexperts as types appear to be equally convincing and equally plausible, their assertions about the future equally unconvincing and equally implausible. It is desired that they have transparent interests and values. Their opinions count because we know what they represent. Negotiations can then be defined as an attempt to increase uncertainty to the point that the only remaining reasonable option is communicating with one another. However, as we do not have the unlimited time that would be required to reach nondistorted agreement, we find ourselves in a quandary.

Responsibility to Ignorance

In an essay strikingly entitled "The Ecology of Ignorance," Luhmann further specifies the place we moderns find ourselves in, one we must take account of, if we are to understand the contemporary world. We move in a situation of systemic ignorance.

60

Some of this ignorance is produced knowingly, but some is not. Precisely because of the form we have given to the future, we find ourselves within an ecology of ignorance. This point does not imply that we need a better map of what we don't know so that we can go about acquiring the requisite knowledge in an ever more comprehensive manner. That task would still fall somewhere between the encyclopedic projects of the Enlightenment (and their nineteenth-century humanistic descendents such as the *Encyclopedia Britannica*) and the modernist projects with their Habermasian "universal norms."[14] Rather, it means that there are inherently volatile, temporally unfolding spaces of ignorance that do not require filling in (as they were not always there and there will always be more of them). These spaces are differentially distributed and are, of course, saturated by partially volatile and partially frozen sets of power relations.

Acknowledging an ecology of (partial and permanent) ignorance would have important consequences. First, it would further deflate the authority of those making futuristic pronouncements—who can remember back less than a decade when debate around mapping the genome turned on the alternatives of the genome as Holy Grail leading to everlasting health versus genomic mapping leading to an inevitable *Back Door to Eugenics?* It is evident now that those making such assertions had no possible knowledge on which to base such claims. Such claims fluctuate between tautologies—the rich will profit from this (whatever the "this" is)—and hype—a new age of medicine is dawning "within a decade." But why is there so much debate about things we cannot know about—now? To pose the question is to answer it. These platitudes and clichés should be seen as attempts to fix reference points for debate and communication. They are part of a sociologically essential hype that prognosticative observers of science and society can now not operate without. Luhmann puts this insight bluntly: "The intensity of ecological communication is based on ignorance. That the future is unknowable is expressed in the present as communication. Society is irritated but has only one way to react to its irritation, in its own manner of operation: communication" (78). Let's hold a conference, set up a commission, have a lively debate, write editorials, take a stance, position ourselves. These activities are often referred to as political or, at times, ethical.

We have a responsibility to our ignorance.[15] Luhmann chooses the philosophy of Hans Jonas as the most sustained attempt to develop an ethics (of procedure and value) in a technological age. Jonas argued that the heart of ethics lies in taking responsibility for the (future) consequences of our actions. This position has two major inherent limitations. First, as we live in a modernity in which the future appears as contingent, the ethical actor cannot know the future chain of consequences of her actions. This situation leads to a dilemma: Either we do not act (but then who takes responsibility for the consequences of inaction?), or we act responsibly knowing that we cannot know what our actions will lead to. For Luhmann this impasse leads to a shift to a rhetoric of communication.[16] That communication is about values. "A normative understanding of values serves to allow an ethics to formulate moral demands for the behavior of others, demands *that can be maintained despite constant disappointments.*" Our contemporary world is peopled with ethical experts whose work is to constantly reassert the importance of core values such as autonomy or dignity. As no one really knows what would count as success empirically given the horror of the current world, the one thing that can be counted on is more discussion: a demand to communicate.

Observing Observers Observing

Luhmann's description of modernity is paradoxical. It is both a description of an epoch—modernity as a period of contingency, functional differentiation, and individualism—and a systematic critique of epochal thinking as realism. Hans Blumenberg argued that in the early nineteenth century there was a shift in the meaning of the term "epoch" from its older meaning of a "point of view" (originally from astronomy) to a totalizing view of the world as historically organized into periods. Reinhart Koselleck also shares the latter claim, arguing that our contemporary sense of historicity emerged precisely at the moment Blumenberg indicates.[17] Blumenberg advocates a return to a form of understanding of epoch as a place from which one looks out at things rather than to continue to pursue realist claims to identify periods that, he argues, can never be empirically justified and only produce an infinite regress of detail and thus futile polemic over boundaries and definitions.

In his essay "Modernity as Contemporary Society," Luhmann indicates that the diacritic best suited to distinguish modernity as an epoch is the one that marks a temporal break with the past.[18] Making a distinction identifies a rupture—it shows us where to look to see that which is taken to be the crucial dimension of the world that, as long as one accepts this particular distinction, has changed forever. Among the distinctions that have been marked as crucial are the birth of historical consciousness, the actualization of political and social freedom, the emergence of a self-reflective subject, the self-understanding of society as risk, the disenchantment of the world, and the triumph of alienation. Each of these different claimants marks modernity differently, although Luhmann points out that each turns on a form of experience associated with a specific understanding of temporality. Luhmann, as we have just seen, has his own candidate—modernity as contingency. Again, however, Luhmann's entire work is at pains to show that the founding distinction of a system is, by definition, arbitrary—in the mathematical sense of the term. This does not mean it is false, but only that once a distinction is drawn it carries with it exclusions and blind spots. A common blind spot is the ability to see the necessity of drawing distinctions and that any clearly drawn distinctions will exclude others. Once one sees and accepts this basic requirement of arbitrariness as the condition of analytic rigor, then systems theory can move in good faith from that arbitrariness to a kind of realism. Luhmann can proceed to give us an epochal description of modernity as contingency, knowing full well that it is arbitrary.

Observing First-order Observers

What is observation? "Observation," Luhmann writes, "is any kind of operation that makes a distinction so as to designate one (but not the other) side. Such a definition is itself contingent, since what is defined would have another meaning given another distinction" (47). Luhmann is giving the term "observation" an idiosyncratic definition; he means by it simply the starting distinction that organizes and begins an inquiry. The starting distinction situates the observer and identifies that which is to be observed. Only then can inquiry proceed. First-order observations thus are ordinary realist attempts to grasp a referent. This type of observation is what most social scientists and most actors in the social world are content to do. It establishes an environment, a point of observation, and a referent. Luhmann draws a distinction between first-order observations and second-order observations. "Observations of the first order (reference) use distinction as a schema but do not yet create a contingency for the observer himself" (47). Second-order observations are observations of first-order observations; they take the system (observer-environment) established by the first-order observations as their referent. By so doing, it becomes possible to take up blind spots that the perfectly legitimate arbitrariness established by the first-order observations. Of course, there is no absolute privilege for any specific second-order observation, as it too is based on making a distinction.

> Second order observations offer a choice [ ] whether certain designations are to be attributed to the observed observer, thereby characterizing him, or seen as characteristics of what he observes. Both attributions, observer attribution and object attribution, are possible; the results can be considered contingent. They can be combined, for example, when an observation is believed to be factually correct but the question remains why the observed observer happens to be interested in this instead of something else. (48)

Thus, first-order observations are directed at one context, or situation, or environment. Second-order observations are directed toward more than one context, situation, or environment; they include the observation of observers observing a context, and the fact that they are observing them.

> Observations of the second order are observations of observations. This can include observations of other observers or observations of the same or different observers at different points in time. Depending on these variants, social and temporal dimensions can be distinguished in the production of meaning. This makes it possible to state that contingency is a form that takes on the factual dimension of the medium of meaning, whereas the social dimension and the temporal dimension pull observation apart. Or to put it another way: everything becomes contingent whenever what is observed depends on who is being observed. (47–48)

Thus one could well observe modernity as an epoch as long as one is aware that a second-order observer observes that starting point as a first-order observation.

Chronicling Observation

It follows that a contemporary anthropologist whose object of study is modern first-order observers must engage in second-order observation. That is to say, set up a frame of inquiry that allows for this double contingency of the first-order observer and the second-order observer. This demand, while complex, is clear once one accepts Luhmann's distinctions. What is less self-evident, but equally logical, is that anthropologists engaged in second-order observations of first-order observers must find a way to take their own observation practice into account. The traditional attempt to do something like this, as we have seen, was to introduce a range of analytic practices aimed at identifying and neutralizing factors that distorted the observational powers of the observer.

Luhmann's analytic helps us to see that there is another way to proceed: "One thing the observer must avoid is wanting to see himself and the world. Only the unity of the distinguished can be observed" (111). In accord with this maxim, anthropologists of the contemporary will find it helpful, perhaps even essential, to include a second (second-order) observer in the practice of anthropological inquiry. Such an observer would have the task to observe the (second-order) observer observing the (first-order) observers. Such an observer would be better than technical devices such as video cameras at recording interview sessions and the like precisely because the second, second-order observer would know that she should not attempt to see herself and the world. Although the possibility of an infinite regress of higher-level observers exists logically, initial experience with the technique indicates that two observers with clearly defined functions are a sufficiently powerful apparatus for the purposes at hand. This apparatus provides safeguards against a belief in the transparency of immediate history.

Original History

Georg Wilhelm Friederich Hegel (1780–1831), at the beginning of his posthumously published lectures, *Introduction to the Philosophy of History*, distinguishes three types of historical writing: original history, reflective history, and philosophic history. Although Hegel is known for his practice of the third kind of historical writing, unexpectedly, his presentation of the first type—original history (*ursprungliche Geschichte*)—today proves to be vivid and relevant to the project of an anthropology of the contemporary. Hegel himself is respectful of original history but thinks it no longer adequate to modern times. The reason is that "Our culture is essentially intellectual, and it immediately converts events into reports for intellectual representation."[19] Modern times are fundamentally mediated by concepts, and the immediacy of war and politics has given way to a more removed and divided situation.

Hegel names the Greek historians as the inventors of original history. These observers

> primarily describe the actions, events, and situations they themselves have witnessed, and whose spirit they shared in. They translate what is externally present into the realm of mental representation, [they] rely on reports and accounts of others, since it is not possible for one person to have seen everything. But they use these sources as ingredients only. [ ] Short spans of time, the individual patterns of men and events—these are the singular, unreflected features out of which he composes his portrait of the time, in order to bring that picture to posterity with as much clarity as it had in his own direct observation or in the accounts of other direct witnesses. He is not concerned with offering reflections on these events, for he lives within the spirit of the times and cannot as yet transcend them.

[T]here are the speeches, which we can read, for example, in Thucydides; these were surely not spoken as they are represented but were worked up by the writer of the history. Speeches, however, are actions among men, and indeed they are effective action in their very essence.[20]

Hegel's distinctions help us to obtain some conceptual distance from the present; for precisely that reason, it is necessary to indicate a few of the differences from Hegel's position. First and foremost, his entire philosophy of the unfolding of Spirit in History is a dead letter. Hegel's assurance that Thucydides lived in a unified epoch, where the culture of Greece formed the element in which all free citizens moved as the proverbial fish in water, and therefore that Thucydides can unproblematically be taken to be a spokesman for this epoch and this culture, is empty. The contemporary pertinence of Thucydides' work is found elsewhere.

Previous generations of scholars would not have been surprised by Hegel's attention to Thucydides, whose *The Peloponnesian War* had for centuries occupied a place in the canon of Greek and Western thought. Today, Thucydides is unknown to most American students and their professors, and my discussion of his work is intended in part to pique their interest. Little is known about this Athenian admiral, member of a noble family; he was probably born around 460 B.C. and probably died in the mid 390s B.C. What is known is that, as the famous opening sentences of *The Peloponnesian War* read, "Thucydides, an Athenian, wrote the war between the Peloponnesians and the Athenians, beginning at the moment that it broke out, and believing that it would be a great war, and more worthy of relation than any that had preceded it. This belief was not without its grounds."[21] The war broke out at the end of the summer in 431, and Thucydides' chronicle finishes at the end of the summer 411 in the war's twenty-first year. Thucydides proposed descriptive accuracy. In

424 B.C. he was sent by Athens to the northern city of Amphipolis to defend it against Spartan attack. He failed. He was exiled. Since I turn to Thucydides in order to mark the existence of a genealogy of writing and thinking about events and their narration, it is appropriate to pay attention to his key terms. Thus, for example, although the standard translation of the first line of his text includes the term "history," the word is not present in the Greek. Thucydides says literally that he "wrote the war."[22] The contrastive cases of "writing things" for Thucydides would be Homer and Herodotus; to their "romance" or "fabulation," at one point he writes, "by reason of my exile, I had leisure to observe affairs more closely." Thucydides' linking of the terms "leisure," "observe," "affairs," and "closely" is significant. The standard translation of these terms is misleading: "leisure" is not the Greek *skholè*, which Pierre Bourdieu has analyzed in detail, but rather "calm." To "observe" is a poor translation of the Greek *aesthesis*, which is better translated as "to be acquainted with (through the senses)." "Affairs" is simply "things," and "more closely" is "better." Hence Thucydides says, "I had the calm to acquaint myself better with things."

Writing Things: Deictic Not Epideictic

A central reason for *The Peloponnesian War* seeming accessibility is the famous speeches (some twenty-seven in all) that Thucydides groups at crucial junctures in his chronicle. Although much scholarly ink has been spilled over the speeches' authenticity and veracity, less incisive reflection has been devoted to the reasons why Thucydides might have included them in his account in the first place. Hegel finds it self-evident that the speeches of Thucydides are present as part of "the spirit of his time." They are instances of "representation," not examples of reflective or critical history. Here is Thucydides' own explanation of why he included the speeches and how they fit in his manner of writing things:

> What was said in speeches by either side, [ ] has been difficult for me to remember exactly in terms of what precisely was spoken (both of what I heard myself or of what was reported to me by others). But as every individual would seem to have said pretty much what he had to concerning the circumstances at hand, so have I written it, staying as close as possible to the entire sense of what was actually spoken. [ ] But both about those events I was witness to and to those I learned of from others, as much as possible I scrutinized everyone [and his account] with a view to accuracy. Even so it was a difficult task to discover [a true account] because participants in events do not agree with each other in their statements, but differed because of their memories [being faulty] or because of their interests in events.[23]

Marc Cogan offers a perspicacious account of the speeches in *The Peloponnesian War* in a book entitled *The Human Thing: The Speeches and Principles of Thucydides' History*.[24] Cogan argues cogently that most of the interpretations of the function of the speeches in Thucydides are misguided. Cogan's core thesis is that the reason Thucydides includes so many speeches, and groups them at key turning points in the long war, is to make visible the functioning of deliberation, in the classical sense of the use of rhetoric to make prudential decisions, during a time of war. Cogan argues that most of the criticisms of Thucydides (as well as many of the interpretations of those who praise him) are misleading because they take the speeches to be an example of *epideictic* rhetoric: a rhetoric of display and embellishment. In this interpretation, the speeches are mere devices through which Thucydides can present his own views through the guise of marionette characters. Cogan vigorously contests this view. Rather, he urges us to take Thucydides literally at his word that he had done his utmost to establish the speeches' accuracy. That accuracy turns not on the representation of a *type* of speech, but— and this is Cogan's thesis—precisely on the *particularity* of the given speech. The interpretive question then becomes how to seize the speeches and their situation in their particularity. Thucydides' challenge is to move from the particular to the general; this motion is an exact inversion of an *epideictic* rhetoric.

Why did Thucydides choose the speeches that he did, given that innumerable speeches had been given during the course of the decades-long war? It is in that selectivity, Cogan argues, that the drive for particularity reveals its significance.[25] His thesis is that these speeches demonstrate the importance of the process of deliberation in shaping the course of the war. The speeches are presented as turning points at which things could have gone in a different direction, ones where significant strategic decisions were taken through the medium of public deliberation either by statesmen addressing the assembled citizenry (as in the famous speeches of Pericles in Athens during the plague) or in dialogues between parties representing their cities (as in the famous Melian dialogue). Discourse in such settings was political action; it was an instantiation of itself, not a representation of something else.

This claim leads us to one further distinctive trait of Thucydides' practice: he presents the speeches not as excerpts but as capturing the timing and affect of the whole speech.

> The practice is, of course, foreign to contemporary historical practice, but we must recognize, novel in Thucydides' time as well. In understanding his purposes in attempting to replicate the complex experience of political oratory on particular occasions, we can discover Thucydides' conceptions of the nature of action that required this form of presentation of the moments of deliberation.[26]

Not only is this foreign to contemporary historical practice, it is foreign to contemporary journalism and to contemporary social science. Each of these forms of narration retains a type of authorial control that does not make the extended process of deliberation available for others to ponder and evaluate for themselves. In that sense these other genres are equally *epideictic;* they use quotation and empirical material essentially to illustrate, reinforce, or embellish a point or to bolster an interpretation or support a theoretical claim. In journalism the genre constraints are such that extended quotation is simply not allowed; journalists are paid to tell the audience what things mean, and editors are paid to police them, that is, to improve their prose so that it thusly functions. In science studies, the primacy of "theory" means that the examples are almost exclusively deployed to strengthen and to demonstrate a theoretical point. Even in the natural sciences, where papers are required to include a methods section, any extended account of deliberative process is absent.

Thucydides is seeking to understand what happened in this long war. While writing, he is no longer an actor in these events; he is in exile but immediately adjacent to things. Thus it seems fair to conclude that he is not writing uniquely, as Hegel argues, in an "immediate" mode, but rather in a mediated mode, one that is unquestionably reflective, while remaining contemporary to the events themselves. No longer a citizen of Athens, but still attached to it by a myriad of other ties and affects (of kinship, of style of thought, or attachment to place), Thucydides, in his presentation of the materials on the war, takes as his object public deliberation and makes it available as an object to ponder, consider, debate—in a word, to consider it as itself an object of deliberation.

✳

VEHEMENT CONTEMPORARIES

The great historian of late antiquity, Peter Brown, opens his splendid book *Poverty and Leadership in the Later Roman Empire* with the statement:

> I wish to draw attention to the social and religious implications of a revolution in the social imagination that accompanied the rise and establishment of the Christian Church in the Roman empire in the late antique period, that is, between the years 300 and 600 of the Common Era. It is a revolution closely associated with the rise to power of the Christian bishop as an increasingly prominent leader in late Roman society. For the Christian bishop was held by contemporaries to owe his position in no small part to his role as guardian of the poor. He was the "lover of the poor" *par excellence:* [ ] // To be a "lover of the poor" became a public virtue. It was a virtue expected of Christian emperors. The *humanitas*, the benevolent style associated with the Roman emperor in the classical period, came to include demonstrative concern for the poor.[1]

Brown's well-documented and richly illustrated claim is that he has identified the emergence of a new moral and social sensibility. This sensibility was neither a simple extension nor a gradual magnification of previous pagan moral sentiments or social ties. "It takes some effort of the historical imagination," Brown writes, "to realize that, around the year 360 C.E. 'love of the poor' was a relatively novel (and for many human and public-spirited persons, still a largely peripheral) virtue." Not only was this sentiment new, but it stood partly in tension with and partly in outright contradiction to previous philanthropic institutions and practices that constituted the virtuous manner of public giving. The very notion of what qualified as the moral bonds of community began to be put in question and challenged. Previously, Brown tells us, "[A] great giver was expected to give to a specific group and to no other: and in the definition of the group, the 'poor,' as such, had no place whatsoever" (3). Rather, it was the civic community—the *demos* or the *populus*—of the city that received the gift, not a category that was fundamentally exotic to these well-to-do and virtue-seeking Romans, the poor. "A rich man was praised for being a *'philopatris*, a lover of the home city, never for being a *philoptochos*, a lover of the poor" (5). The rich conceived of themselves as belonging to a distinctive community, the city.

The gradual emergence and slow, if unrelenting, spread of a core Christian and Jewish understanding of charity over time eventually produced a new community: "To act as a 'lover of the poor' was to make an assertion, heavy with symbolic meaning, of one's acknowledgment of the ultimate cohesion of the entire human community" (6). The formation of new moral imaginaries is an unusual event, important in and of itself, but if it is to form an integral part of an enduring community—and thereby challenge traditional moral bonds—then those who seek to implement these imaginaries must seriously attend to power relations and what is now called institution-building. Brown draws a vivid picture of how the central figure of the bishop came to be supported fiscally by the Christian community and how their new governmental obligations gradually took shape during the course of the ensuing centuries, thereby substantially but not completely displacing older understandings and institutions.

Although this shift in the object of moral sentiment and the institutions and actors upon which it depended extended to the entire human community, Brown shows that there were two major exceptions to its scope that endured for centuries and centuries. The first concerned slaves, who fell outside the circle of humanity; the care of the poor was an obligation only by and for free persons. "Although slaves were seen as objects of compassion by Christians," Brown writes, "they were not considered to have destinies, as free persons did, for which the bishop and the clergy might consider themselves to be responsible" (61). The second exception or limit to the equality of beings within the human community was God. There was a "vertical [ ] relationship between God and his believer. Every believer was to God what the beggar was to the giver of alms—a being utterly dependent on the mercy of another" (86). Still, the Christian God had descended to Earth, and his son had died for the sins of the human community. Brown shows that the mystery of why God had instantiated himself in the Christ was explained doctrinally to the flock with the claim that "Only a God who, in becoming Christ, had taken into his very being the thirst and hunger of humankind, could with *perfect sincerity*, condemn the rich for lack of fellow feeling for the poor" (111). Only thus—in all sincerity—could the Last Judgment be conducted validly and with appropriate affect.

There are many things to be said about Brown's richly textured account, but of direct relevance here are the identification of sentiment, emotion, passion and affect as core dimensions of moral claims; that such claims are embedded in relationships; that there are actors whose role is to articulate and embody those moral claims, sentiments, and affects in their practices. It is also important to note that although Brown took as his theme the identification of the rise and spread of one such moral apparatus, his book eloquently testifies to the fact that the other, in this case older, apparatuses (with their moral claims, affects, actors, practices, and the like) did not simply disappear from the face of the Earth in a seismic epochal jolt. Rather, there was a long series of historical changes in which more than one set of apparatuses were operating, and within each there were contestations over the meaning of claims, over what constituted an appropriate sentiment, over how to modulate the accompanying affect, as well as over who exactly was the right social actor to bring forth and carry out the Christian message. The Protestant Reformation after all was directed against Rome and its agents. Finally, today many of these quite ancient claims to moral insight and mood are recognizable, as are even some of the sentiments and affects associated with them. There is another story to tell of a long history of aggregation and disaggregation of each of the elements of these apparatuses and the shifting relationships among and between them.

One example that will figure prominently in our story is "sincerity." The literary critic Lionel Trilling defines the term in his classic book *Sincerity and Authenticity*, as follows:

> If sincerity is the avoidance of being false to any man through being true to one's self, one can see that this state of personal existence is not to be attained without the most arduous effort. And yet at a certain point in history, certain men and classes of men conceived that the making of this effort was of supreme importance to the moral life and the value they attached to the enterprise of sincerity became a salient, perhaps a definitive, characteristic of Western culture for some four hundred years.[2]

Trilling does not dwell on the Christian connection that Peter Brown insisted upon because Trilling's real interest is the decline of a distinctive relationship or, more accurately, of a double relationship: the duplexity is put most famously in the celebrated advice Polonius gave to his son in *Hamlet:* "This above all, to thine own self be true, and it does follow as the night upon the day, Thou canst not be false to any man." Thus there is a chain:

there is the relationship to the self, and the work required to achieve it, and there is the work on one's relationship to others that flows, it is held, effortlessly once the first labors have been accomplished. The core thesis of Trilling's book is that the latter half of this chain has been severed from the former half; being true to oneself had been disembedded from its connections with one's relationship to others. Moderns hold, Trilling claims, that one should be true to oneself, not to be true to others, but rather to achieve authenticity. This shift has not led to a rampant increase of sanctioned falsehood to others, "only that it does not figure as the defining purpose of being true to one's self."[3] In fact the semantics have almost reversed themselves: if being true to oneself serves the goal of being true to others, then it is a mere means and not an end in itself. Moderns seek to display a sincere self in public for its own sake.

Trilling opened his book with a claim that again brings Peter Brown to mind. "Now and then it is possible to observe the moral life in process of revising itself, perhaps by reducing the emphasis it formerly placed upon one or another of its elements, perhaps by inventing and adding to itself a new element, some mode of conduct or of feeling which hitherto it had not regard as essential to virtue."[4] While there do seem to be watershed moments in sensibility, especially if one is referring to a restricted set of literary texts as Trilling does, much else in his epochal claims rings flat, even exotic, today. Perhaps that response arises in part, and there is a certain irony in this, from the fact that modes of conduct or feeling appear less settled today than they did three decades ago when Trilling was writing and the Western world seemed rife with epochal change. Whether this current sense of stasis or even retrogression exists because the moral life is once again in process of revising itself, or because the way actions and judgments are observed, recorded, and modulated has shifted, or whether there simply is no unitary thing that the signifier "the moral life" signifies, is hard to say.

77

My hypothesis is that no single sensibility—modernist or otherwise—dominates, overarches, or underlies current affairs. Rather, one can observe a mangle of practice that includes sentiment, emotion, passion, and affect. One reason for my claim is that the concept of culture as either the unified way of life of a people or the dominant sensibility of its elite, or its oppressed, is no longer among the concepts attributed analytic acuity by those authorized to do so. This essay is not the place to tell the story of the decline of the culture-concept.[5] Let us say here that the "elements" that Trilling cites—or those cited by Peter Brown or others soon to be presented—can be, and have been, combined and recombined in numerous ways, and that these manners of affiliation, coupling, decoupling, assembling, and the like are themselves quite diverse. Again, this claim does not mean that there are not attempts to unify these elements and their combinations, to codify them, to find their unities, or to despair of coherence altogether, but only that all such efforts themselves constitute grist for the anthropological mill.

Rugged Terrain

There exists a vast literature on the moral vocabulary, practices, and principles appropriate to an ever-growing list of present day issues characterized as "moral" or "ethical." It seems self-evident to the majority of the producers of this specialized literature that it is the pressing problems in need of clarification and resolution that occasioned the moral dilemmas, paradoxes, ironies, and contradictions. Furthermore, it appears self-evident to those authorized to pronounce serious speech acts on such matters that it should—nay must—be possible to address these problems in a manner that would provide guidance for others in the conduct of their affairs, or at the very least should help to frame the issues in such a way that public discussion and debate could proceed toward clarification and eventual resolution. Despite the oft-repeated need for the discovery of such a set of moral principles, upon investigation one observes that no such discovery has ever taken place in a manner that is stable.

The contemporary moral landscape is heterogeneous. One observes a proliferation of types and figures of moral discourse—held to be incompatible by first-order observers—both within collectivities and even within individuals: divergent ethical and epistemological discourses multiply; actors frequently, perhaps always, employ more than one. This state of affairs frequently troubles those in search of consistency understood as internal logical rigor, one aspect of the process Max Weber referred to as "rationalization." In their trouble, however, such actors often contribute to the process of rationalization. However, others active in the same systematization process but producing systems based in different ethical substances will not be convinced by logical rigor alone.

The way that the moral landscape is inhabited in daily life (including moments of crisis or rupture) is logically disjunctive from the moral landscape as reflected upon by those authorized to pronounce prescriptive speech acts about it. Thus, while many of the serious speech acts about the moral landscape are produced by actors who are reflective about their own positions, the anthropologist can approach their discourses and practices like those of any other. Theorists, philosophers, ethicists, scientists, and the like can thus qualify for inclusion in the category that used to be called "natives." No contemporary moral debates of any import have been resolved through disputation and argumentation alone. Although this observation should probably be troubling to a philosopher in search of universals without which a grounded moral life is held to be impossible, to an anthropologist the lack of consensus and/or resolution does not mean that nothing of significance is happening or that people are not leading ethical lives. Rather, it points to the need for more thoughtful anthropological inquiry into what the Icelandic anthropologist Gisli Palssón has astutely labeled "the moral landscape."

Elements of a Contemporary Moral Landscape

There are at least three major archaeological layers that function as genealogical vectors in the contemporary moral landscape. As a first crude approximation, one finds empirically:

1. A constant recourse to one or another of the diverse and complexly structured traditions of what has been referred to as the Greek and the Judeo-Christian. There are constant references to the vocabulary of Christian vices and virtues (greed, humility, pride); and to the ethical categories of the philosophical tradition (flourishing, dispassionate observation, ambition, anger, excellence).

2. A frequent invocation of the modern wellsprings of procedural- and principle-based reasoning as the basis for judgment. These include the dominance of bioethical and biomedical discourses by the Kantian form of ethics as well as the widespread use of one or another variant of a Habermasian communication ethics seeking clarification and consensus. The form of these discourses is appropriate to bureaucratic bodies charged with management of institutions. Of course the plurality of value systems or life worlds or multiculturalism is recognized by its advocates, but the problem is precisely how to manage such diversity in the name of the right and the fair. Reinhart Koselleck has provided an especially useful tool in his corpus of *Begriffsgeschichte*, or conceptual history. Almost all the terms he and his team consider are modern (secular) ones; they provide a rich social, political, and semantic contextualization for the concepts articulation and deployment. Such contextualization does not undermine their force or utility, although it does render them historical and thus

contingent. This loosening is helpful when terms are claimed to be universal and/or ahistorical. That is to say, it provides a further second-order analytic.

3. A blustery or quietly troubled dissatisfaction with both of the above vectors as either appropriate to or comprehensive of the problems and issues of life today. It is clear that there are many practices around today that can be described by the older vocabularies of virtue ethics and/or moral principle, but it is also clear that if one looks in detail and conducts anthropological inquiry into the matter, there is much that overflows these categories. Hence one finds an oft-repeated call to invent new terms, new modes, new forms of describing and evaluating. Although Hans Blumenberg, Niklas Luhmann, Gilles Deleuze, and Michel Foucault have all contributed to identifying a problematic, their contributions remain propaideutic.

There are ardent practitioners of each of the above lines of figuration who argue strenuously—and with recurrent and recursive (first-order) futility—for their adequacy and appropriateness. An anthropology of the contemporary moral landscape notes that such practices and beliefs are most certainly relevant for the study of *Wissenschaft und Lebensführung*.

Genomics as Ethical Terrain

Today, who is authorized to speak the truth about life? The answer is both straightforward and complex. The straightforward aspect of the answer is that in the early twenty-first century in the United States and Western Europe (as well as several other countries that would be worth mapping), it is practitioners of the life sciences and their medical colleagues who are authorized to speak the truth about life. There are, however, other domains than the scientific where parallel claims are put forth but arise from a different source of authority and within a different frame of coherence; for example, there is currently a fundamentalist Protestant revival taking place in the United States; or the Catholic Church formally declaims its views with regularity, as do other religious denominations.[6] Many American scientists are themselves religious practitioners. In that sense, Max Weber's trenchant admonition to German university students in his 1917 essay "Science as a Vocation," that science (*Wissenschaft*) can pose questions but can provide no answers as to the fundamental questions of the meaning of existence, would find a chorus of accord from a choir of practitioners who Weber clearly did not have in mind. Many, as we shall see, are quite comfortable with this division of labor.

As anthropologists we can proceed with a description that says there is a group of people who have been invested with authority to make claims about what is known about life processes. Whether they are molecular biologists, genomics specialists, proteomics experts, or bio-informaticians, the group can be broadly identified. What is the moral basis—if any—that those authorized to speak the truth about life processes invoke? What moral authority do scientists claim? What moral authority do scientists rely on? What kind of moral authority does the public expect? Is there a necessary supplement to sheer technical or scientific insight or skill? It seems clear that whatever may be the status of the ethical standing of the knowledge-producer within the authorized spheres of the academy and industry, the issue of "Who speaks?" remains alive for the larger public. The vast domain of popular writing, film making, and artistic production devoted to these topics is beyond my ken. What I do have anthropological experience with—and this is one of the major underanalyzed aspects of the genome mapping projects—is the constant deployment of a moral language comparing and contrasting the major scientific players who conceived, articulated, and drove the project to fruition. One dimension of this fact is perhaps simple: these are highly competitive men (almost entirely) seeking fame, power, and glory. It would be normal that they would elide the language of morals in their "mad pursuit," in Francis Crick's famous phrase, of truth and power.

But they don't—and that fact is worth pondering. The manner in which this rhetoric is deployed is of prime importance. For an anthropologist the moral rhetoric of praise and blame is especially interesting because many of the main actors are themselves remarkably unrestrained and crude in their manner of announcing judgments. They feel fully authorized to speak their mind, and to do so in an ordinary vernacular that shocks and pleases. In fact, they employ a rhetoric of authenticity. Although few would have been competent to judge the claims to the impossibility of "whole genome shotgun sequencing" in 1998—a time when no one could scientifically answer the question as to the capacity of the untested technique—it is not difficult to decipher the intent and meaning of a statement from a Nobel laureate when he accuses an opponent of performing a "con job" and this vulgarity is published in the most prestigious of scientific journals; or when another Nobel laureate repeatedly refers to an opponent as "Hitler" at sanctioned meetings of elite scientists, many of whom are funded by the federal government. Such unblushing offensiveness is a feast for the anthropologist. How calculated is its deployment? Why that vocabulary? In a word, the topic of inquiry here is initial mappings of the moral landscape of genomic scientists and their public in the late twentieth and early twentieth-first century.

These musings bring us to the terrain of the "moral" and the "ethical." The very existence of such a poorly demarcated domain, and the rather heterogeneous and amorphous entry qualifications authorizing those who participate in it—not to mention the curious fact that it exists at all—is arresting. Its privileged existence is especially worthy of note in one of the most litigious societies in the history of the world. This essay is not the place to review the history of post–World War II ethics any more than it was the decline of the concept of culture.[7] Hence, for the present a few signposts of the emergence and institutionalization of bioethics will have to suffice. A further claim, of course, is that a range of moral sensibility is changing—and that we are in crying need of analytic tools more adequate than "epoch" and "culture" or "sensibility" to address that complex shift.

Agon in the Genomic Terrain

Although the race to sequence the human genome produced competition of a vigorous and ruthless sort, no one has been formally charged with illegal conduct in a court of law. In contrast, the techno-scientific terrain has provided fertile ground for plausible charges of moral high- and low-handedness, character flaws, and ethical compromise to flourish. These conditions are, of course, related. All the institutions engaged in the contest—government, industry, academy, philanthropy, and media—employ lawyers. The one arena, however, in which these highly paid lawyers seem to be called upon to represent their clients in formal legal settings is that of patent law. And even in questions of patent law there is a good deal of adjacent space where claims and counterclaims are made as to who is behaving properly or improperly; a space where innuendo precedes, accompanies, and follows upon the conduct of legal proceedings strictly defined. The emergence of a significant public space of the "ethical" is one of the most distinctive events in social history over the last several decades: its discourse and institutions occupy a seemingly ever-expanding space carved out between the legal and the political.

The completion of the project to sequence the human genome was by any standards a technological triumph and a scientific landmark. It also became widely publicized as a "race" to finish the job first, although exactly what that meant was never very clear. Most readers will have some memory of the media event staged by President Clinton and Prime Minister Blair at the White House Rose Garden in June 2000 to celebrate the achievement. High-level international political intervention had resulted in an agreement for the competitors in the "race" to sequence the human genome to cross the finish line together. Who were the competitors? The public project grouped the National Institutes of Health, the Department of Energy, multiple university laboratories receiving federal grants to carry out the sequencing work, the world's largest philanthropy (the Wellcome Trust in Britain), as well as smaller publicly funded genome projects from diverse countries (U.K., France, Japan, Germany, and China). The public consortium was pitted against Celera Genomics, a biotech company located in Rockville, Maryland. The public project was represented by Francis Collins, a geneticist who had been codiscoverer of the "cystic fibrosis gene" (for which he was co-inventor of a patent) before becoming director of the National Institutes of Health Human Genome Project, and the private one was represented by Craig Venter, an outspoken maverick of the scientific world and chief scientific officer of Celera Genomics. Venter had previously worked for the NIH and made his name, and many enemies, by attempting to patent stretches of DNA known as Expressed Sequence Tags when he worked at NIH, even though their biological function was unknown, a prospect many considered to be scandalous.

Both the public project and Celera portrayed the importance of the attempt to sequence the human genome in epic terms. Addressing scientists assembled at the Mecca of molecular biology, Cold Spring Harbor Laboratory, Collins had said, "I hope this doesn't sound corny or grandiose [ ] but I feel this [ ] is the most important scientific effort that humankind has ever mounted."[8] After achieving one milestone along the way, Sir John Sulston, head of the British project, called the achievement "as important an accomplishment as discovering that the Earth goes around the Sun, or that we are descended from apes." Venter was quoted as saying: "We're going to establish a new paradigm, we're going to prove you can do open research and make money at the same time."[9] Each of these men craved publicity, and each was relentlessly competitive: Venter reveled in his bad-boy reputation, while Collins consistently promoted himself as "selfless," and Sulston seemed convinced that he had been designated to defend humanity perhaps by the Goddess of Reason.

James Shreeve, a scientific journalist, has written a riveting account of this "race" to sequence the human genome. He gives us an extraordinary blow by blow—or perhaps cell phone by cell phone—narrative of how both the technological and moral battles were staged and fought. Shreeve had untrammeled access to Celera during the whole course of the events. He had much less access to the public project, whose representatives not only politely refused to let him observe their meetings but blocked significant portions of the public record that Shreeve sought access to through a Freedom of Information Act request. This fact, which comes only at the end of the book in a "Note on Sources," is a shock. Shreeve dryly observes that he was told by "the head of NIH's FOIA office that they were permitted to deny access under Exemption 4 of the FOIA, which prevents the release of 'commercial and financial information that is privileged and confidential.' Considering the concerted efforts the HGP leaders made during the race to distinguish their totally free, totally public version of the genome from Celera's commercial one, the explanation sounds oddly discordant."[10] Having read that far in the book, the reader will have abandoned any illusions that this was a combat between knights in white armor.

As no one else will ever again have such access to the players during the unfolding of the struggle, Shreeve's book should be read by all concerned by the conditions under which science is practiced today. There are accounts defending the public side; John Sulston has already written one, *The Common Thread: A*

Story of Science, Politics, Ethics, and the Human Genome, with Georgina Ferry that tells the story unabashedly from his perspective, and a moral tale of good and evil, pride and modesty, science and politics, it is.[11]

It comes as no surprise, therefore, that the duel to achieve a technological goal was accompanied by a rhetoric of moral combat marked by ferocity and fueled by righteousness and ego. A typical comment is one Collins made at a congressional hearing: "Many in the scientific community are concerned about a circumstance where large amounts of this critical information might, in some way, be constrained from utilization by everybody who wants to use it. It is such *basic* information, and the notion that it would, in some way, be moving out of a public domain enterprise into a single private company has raised some cautions in the minds of many advisors."[12]

Although the emphasis is on "basic," it probably should have been on "single." As the *The Genome War* recounts at length, the personal battles were above all about credit, personal credit. Among the many virtues of the book is its adept chronicling of the complex alliances and strains in those alliances that existed on both sides. On the Celera side, the differences (sometimes minor and sometimes major) between the idiosyncratic and provocative Craig Venter and his boss, the no-nonsense businessman Tony White ("he wears his capitalism on his sleeve"), is clearly set out. Venter's commitment to make the genomic data available—with a delay—came into increasing tension with White's business strategy. This conflict was exacerbated by the tactics of the public project, which constantly painted Celera as betrayers of humankind (James Watson was fond of referring to Venter as "Hitler"[13]) and incompetent scientists whose sequencing strategy would never work—Sulston told *Science* that Venter was involved in a "con job." The tension within the camps and between the camps was also heightened by the (little known) fact that while providing a steady stream of righteous moralism to its academic troops and the media, the public project contracted with the California biotech company Incyte Pharmaceuticals, which was all the while busy patenting genomic information and selling it to a handful of major pharmaceutical companies. In fact, Incyte was a better example of the dangers of mixing commerce and science than was Celera. In 1999, Incyte's CEO Randy Scott announced "that Incyte scientists had hard evidence that there were 140,000 genes in the human genome—twice Venter's estimate and far in excess of the 100,000 figure cited by most researchers. The announcement ignited a rash of national news stories."[14] One of the many things learned from the sequencing to date is that there are more like 22,000 to 26,000 genes, although these may encode a much large number of proteins.

There is an almost Shakespearean quality to the narrative (although perhaps the *Sopranos* is a better fit) as we see Collins and his allies relentlessly performing their sanctimonious Boy Scout cheerleading in public. "The Human Genome Project, Collins told himself, was about community, about the rules that applied to all, about the sacrifice of individual motives for the collective good. It was even a bit about God."[15] Or, "[T]he success in cloning the cystic fibrosis gene brought Collins fame, grant money, and a share of the patent on the gene. [ ] It also brought him closer to God. 'If you drew a circle around what God knows, it would be unimaginably huge,' he later said. 'What I know is a teeny, teeny dot within the circle.'"[16] Shreeve documents at great length how Collins and his loyalists, while defending Humanity, God, and Science, simultaneously engaged behind the scenes in politics most venal—threatening journalists and distinguished scientists, stooping to vulgar name-calling, reneging on agreements, refusing compromises proposed by other government officials.

While early sections of the book fall into an overwritten and breathless style that science journalism frequently adopts, once the narrative pace picks up Shreeve is masterful in keeping the chronicle in constant motion while providing sufficient explanation for the reader to grasp the technological challenges and scientific import of events. Those curious about what "whole genome shotgun" means will find out in plain English. Shreeve presents the moral and political events in all their rawness. The reader comes away informed, if shaken.

Initially, the anthropologist came away shaken as well but was then overtaken by a curiosity about how best to think about these knowledge-seekers and their life ways. Was there really more to say than here were a group of alpha males driven by a lust for money, fame, and power? Was there anything more to this affair than a group of shameless and base types whose names were in the press because of the importance of the project and the need for science journalists to personalize things? I believe that there is more at stake and more to think about. The thin red line between valuations—the sense that the moral assemblage is complexly molded and deployed—is captured by Shreeve in the following lengthy quote:

In retrospect, the beauty of the *Drosophila* project [ ] was that its relatively modest objective allowed it to unfold beneath the radar of history. People could interact unselfishly because no one was competing for a Nobel Prize, much less a niche in heaven next to Mendel, Darwin, Watson, and Crick. The human genome was another matter. Craig Venter wanted to be remembered for doing great things, and saw no reason why he shouldn't admit to this aspiration. In contrast, the leaders of the Human Genome Project insisted that their motives were, to use one of Francis Collins's favorite words, "selfless." Collins and his colleagues defined themselves as defenders of the public interest against a corporation, and a man, bent on selling for profit what was rightfully the shared heritage of all humankind. Constantly drawing attention to one's selflessness

89

is a bit of an oxymoron. But if the human code really was in peril of being privatized, then it is understandable that the HGP scientists would see themselves as "wearing the white hat." On the other hand, if Venter were to receive the recognition he so desperately wanted, he would have to deliver the genome to the world, just as he had promised. So was it the genome that the government scientists wanted to keep out of his grasp, or the credit for capturing it?[17]

The quote points to a series of key features of the complex topography of the current moral terrain. Let us take a look at just a few.

Thumós: Appropriate Anger

All the players who appear in the accounts of the genome war are ambitious. A Web dictionary defines ambitious as "A strong feeling of wanting to be successful in life and achieve great things." Craig Venter is ambitious. Francis Collins is ambitious. Eric Lander is ambitious. John Sulston is ambitious. And, as many wags have observed behind the scenes, only three names can appear on a Nobel Prize. Ambition—like power, beauty, truth, and the good—can be an end in itself. From ancient times personal ambition has been both admired and criticized. For a Greek or Roman in the ancient world, one would not need to justify attempts to do great deeds. Excellence was an end in itself, an end that life at its best strives toward. It was an essential part of "the human thing," to use a striking expression of Thucydides.[18] Great deeds line the road to immortality; it was completely understandable to act so that one day people would sing praise tales of one's achievements. All too aware of where the excesses of ambition could lead, the Greeks and Romans developed a rich analytic vocabulary, primarily an ethical and political one, through which ambition could be thought about, evaluated, and judged.

The striving for great works, praise, and remembrance has been marginalized as a moral virtue by Christianity (following in the wake of Stoicism, which sought to dampen all strong passions), although neither the striving nor the valuation has disappeared.[19] What, therefore, is wrong with ambition? From a Christian perspective, humility is a virtue and its corresponding sin is pride. "Pride is excessive belief in one's own abilities that interferes with the individual's recognition of the grace of God. It has been called the sin from which all others arise" (the thin line between righteousness and self-righteousness). Today, to be legitimate, at least in certain domains (science, art, politics), it appears to be mandatory to cast ambition as a means toward other ends. The modern world has seen the emergence and proliferation of a new figure: in Joseph Conrad's phrase, "the reproachless knight of altruism."[20] We inhabit a world of figures working ever so diligently at what Baudelaire called "the soul's sacred prostitution." That is to say, it is acceptable to pursue achievement and glory as long as it is publicly buttressed and justified by other motives, selfless ones. One must serve humanity. One must serve the good. One must serve the truth. Today, ambition must be "at the service of" if one is to receive one's due among the high-minded. Such projects of collective achievement for advancement and improvement may well be fine and occasionally salutary (that is, useful or promoting good health), but they significantly narrow the discursive space of what Kenneth Burke called "the rhetoric of motives." Therefore, it follows that an ever-increasing swath of human behavior is coded as fallen, discordant, distorted, and inappropriate.

For example, it is surprising to read that an English translator (W. D. Ross) of Aristotle's *Nicomachean Ethics* uses the Christian term "pride" in book 4, chapter 3. The editor, Richard McKeon, provides a footnote to inform the reader that the Greek term is *megalopsukhia* or "greatness of soul," not "pride." Translating *megalopsukhia* as "pride" is not flat out wrong: the Christian sin of pride no doubt could be connected, with appropriate mediations, to the term *hubris* among the Greeks, but then a different tonality and a different range of situations would have to be taken into account. The Greeks held those with "greatness of soul" in the highest esteem. And because they did, they produced a sophisticated set of reflections on what this condition consisted in, what forms it could take, what its virtues were, and how it could become corrupt.

"Anger" frequently appears in that literature as a natural (today we would say normal) accompaniment to the disposition of the great-souled person. Anger had an extraordinary—to us—centrality in the ancient world. For example, it is given careful attention by both Plato and Aristotle. As scholars have documented, there is a large and long-standing classical Greek vocabulary for what we call anger.[21] The terms were frequently bodily ones. Gradually they shifted to a more complicated semantic range, one that, while remaining anchored in the body and its states, gradually focused more on the soul and complex human relations. It was only much later, essentially with the Stoic philosophers, that states of anger as well as other strong passions became the object of an increasingly sophisticated therapeutic vocabulary and technology that sought to tame or even to obliterate them altogether. Of course such states have not been obliterated in human relations, but their place within sanctioned discourses has been marginalized.

The Greek term "*thumós*" is a good example to use for the current discussion. The minimal definition of *thumós* is "spiritedness." For Plato, spiritedness constituted one of the three parts of the soul along with the rational (or calculating) and the appetitive. *Thumós* is closely linked with valuation, anger, and justice. Thus, in book 4 of *The Republic*, Socrates proposes that the nobler a man is—the higher he values his own worth—the angrier he will become when he has been dealt with unjustly.

> But when a man believes himself to be wronged? Does not his spirit in that case seethe and grow fierce [ ] and make itself the ally of what he judge just? And in noble souls it endures and wins the victory and will not let go until either it achieves its purpose, or death ends all, or, as a dog is called back by a shepherd, it is called back by the reason within and calmed.[22]

In the remaining parts of book 4, Plato has Socrates with his interlocutors explore the interplay of reason, appetite, and spiritedness.

Aristotle treats *thumós* in his treatises on rhetoric and ethics. He refers to *thumós* as a principle of high spirit and then immediately associates it with anger. *Thumós* is the capacity of the soul to manifest anger and zeal. *Thumós* is closely connected to the value one sets on oneself as well as the manner in which others respond to that esteem. These definitional conditions lead directly to considerations of justice, politics, and ethics. For example, in the *Rhetoric*, Aristotle's says "anger may be defined as an impulse accompanied by distress, to a conspicuous revenge for a conspicuous slight directed without justification towards what concerns one-self or towards what concerns one's friends" (*Rhetoric* 2.2). We see that we are dealing with a complex state, one arising out of and then plunging immediately back into a complex situation of human relations, traditions, codes of valuation, all of which cannot be reduced to a biological urge, psychological drive, or flux in the modern interiority of the self.

Book 4 of the *Nicomachean Ethics* treats "even-temperedness" or "gentleness" and its excesses and deficits. "The man who is angry at the right things and with the right people, and further, as he ought, when he ought, and as long as he ought, is praised. This will be a good-tempered man" (*Ethics* 4.5). As with the other virtues, the mean is flanked by two equally negative extremes, one an excess, the other a defect. The excess term is "irascibility," but there is no term for the deficit. "Such a man is thought not to feel things nor to be pained by them, and, since he does not get angry, he is thought unlikely to defend himself; and to endure being insulted and put up with insults to one's friends is slavish" (*Ethics* 4.5)). For Aristotle one might say: without *thumós* there are no free citizens; without *agon* no excellence.[23]

Two recent books, written by two quite different authors, have paid sustained attention to *thumós*. The first is Francis Fukuyama's *The End of History and the Last Man*, and the other is by Philip Fisher's *The Vehement Passions*. They provide a convergent diagnosis of the current age, and each, albeit for quite different motives, underscores the current desirability of rethinking and renovating the pre-Christian ethical vocabulary. For both, and this is where their discussions join our own, such exploration cannot possibly be a return to a world long past—Fukuyama is a neoconservative, not a reactionary, and Fisher is a postdeconstructionist, not a postmodern—but rather must function as a source from which one might invent a richer analytics of the contemporary moral terrain.

Following the lead of the French Hegel scholar Alexandre Kojève, Fukuyama equates *thumós* with the Hegelian concept of "the desire for recognition" and with Nietzsche's "beast with red cheeks."[24] What these disparate authors and disparate concepts do share is an emphasis on the active need to "place *value* on things—himself in the first instance, but on the people, actions, or things around him as well" (163). Without affirmation, humans are slavish drones; as Nietzsche puts it, "Man does not strive after happiness; only the Englishman does that" (181). Thus, *thumós* (in this admittedly modern interpretation) is the drive to assign value and the associated and consequent desire for recognition. This striving for value is an activity that entails another consciousness to share or reject the valuation put forth in practice or asserted in discourse. For Fukuyama, following Kojève, *thumós* is something like an innate human sense of justice: people believe that they have a certain worth, and when other people do not recognize their worth at its correct value, then anger arises. The arousal of anger in such circumstances is perfectly appropriate. The intimate relationship between self-evaluation and anger can be seen in the English word "indignation." Fukuyama identifies *thumós* as "the most specifically political part of the human personality because it is what drives men to want to assert themselves over other men" (163). Casting politics in this mode does not prejudge what form that politics might or should take.

Following Plato, Fukuyama rehearses the arguments of the different ways in which *thumós* can be made to ally with desire or with rationality. For Fukuyama—and this is the specific contribution that his book seeks to make—it is *thumós* that can provide the diacritic of the ethical limits to the current overvaluation, the excess of the desirable and/or the calculative. Fukuyama is proposing an updated conservative critique of capitalism and consumerism. In this sense, Fukuyama is a neoconservative: he sees an imbalance in modern society; there has been an overweening economization of life driven by desire for things as well as a tyranny of calculative rationality. These criticisms of modern capitalism are not new and do not need rehearsing here; what is significant is the proposal of introducing *thumós* as a counterbalance, as an essential component of the good life in the Greek sense of a life worth living, a life that flourishes.

Philip Fisher's *The Vehement Passions* presents a much more detailed and nuanced case for renewed attention to the ethics of Plato and especially Aristotle. Fisher argues that we have lost the vocabulary to name and to make flourish the vehement passions: anger, fear, grief, shame. The Greeks saw them as vital goods and we should as well, Fisher argues, because they contain a power to reveal the beauty and power of the world, a capacity to describe—and affirm—a strenuous and event-filled form of life worth living. Finding a plausible means of doing so will not be easy. As opposed to authors like Alasdair MacIntrye, however, who merely lament the loss of such virtues in the modern world and argue that they are gone forever, Fisher is at pains to show that the states of existence named by the ethical vocabulary of Aristotle still remain present in modern life; even if they have become marginal and even if we have lost an affirmative manner of noting them, encouraging them, and practicing them, they have not disappeared.

Fisher proposes to dig back behind millennia of contrary or partially contrary approaches that have muted or silenced the importance and even the existence of the vehement passions. "The passions, as one of the longest uninterrupted, most intricate and necessary descriptive problems in the intellectual life of Western culture, have had time to accumulate waves of damage both from absent words and from the bad surplus of overlapping, once technical, but now informal, vocabulary."[25] He presents a genealogy of outright obliteration or attempts to tame these passions and the types of experience and relations that they emerged from and affirmed. Such an account will be familiar to those who have read Norbert Elias or the recent remarks of Peter Sloterdijk on *"apprivoisment."*[26] For example, as a means to mark the distance from the ancient world, Fisher notes that Hume, whom he admires as having written "the last great treatise on the passions," nonetheless conceives of self-worth as a "settled and expansive pleasure" and by so doing "marks out a profound difference from Greek thought, where that same self-worth is conceived most powerfully in moments where it is challenged by an opposing force."[27] The real turning point, that behind which one must search, is marked by the rise and articulation of what Fisher calls the Stoic assault on the passions. This assault served to make it possible to imagine a conception of human nature only partially present in any one of its states, even the state of dying. Stoic character, or the ideal of the Reasonable Man, as Marcus Aurelius described him, displays to us the essence of that new norm of character. The reasonable man of the Stoics holds himself always partly in reserve. Such a self overlaps with its situations while remembering that it is distinct from them. It seeks to return to itself and agrees to participate only grudgingly in its own states. [ ] By erecting a notion of character that is mainly violated by states of variability, the Stoics could imagine immunity to situations as one of the highest ethical goals. (49)

Living and dying as we do amidst the ministrations of bureaucracies, encountering a range of strangers in daily life or at the bedside in David Rothman's telling phrase, navigating through the labyrinth of an impersonal legal system, surely leaves a place for this Stoic practice of imagined immunity. That place, however, if it becomes the core of a way of life, does indeed seem shrunken in its vehemence and perhaps even in its care.

Again, this is not the place to explore the content of these arguments. A few examples, however, will indicate the fecundity of Fisher's explorations and proposals. Thus, he points out—and this rings true as a proverbial bell—that as anger arises in situations of contested worth, it should not be surprising that anger concerns mainly those one already knows, although not necessarily those with whom one is friends (although anger at friends exists, it may take a different form). The reason for this location is that anger frequently erupts at a point in a series of encounters and events where relations had previously been formed, expectations established, contestations carried out, limits defended or violated. Anger is revelatory, and consequently paying careful attention to it would seem to be well worth the anthropologist's while. Or to take another example: Fisher points out that the topic of weakness of the will, or *akrasia*, has been debated by philosophers (and others) for millennia. Aristotle identified two different aspects of *akrasia:*

> But there are two forms of *akrasia*, Impetuousness or Weakness. The weak deliberate, but then are prevented by passion from keeping to their resolution; the impetuous are led by passion because they do not stop to deliberate. It is the quick and excitable who are most liable to the impetuous form because the former are too hasty and the latter too vehement to wait for reason, being prone to follow their imagination [*phantasia*].[28]

Surely an analysis of the strategies, battles, and encounters between figures like Venter and Collins would be enlightened by the introduction of concepts like *akrasia* and *thumós*.

Vehement Contemporaries

Although only a scattering of scholars have pondered the existence of this situation of archaeological simultaneity, or genealogical heterogeneity, or cotemporal regimes of discourse, or discordant apparatuses, or competing machinic activity, those who have taken up the phenomenon have approached it as being either anomalous or residual, or most commonly as exemplifying a situation of moral nihilism characteristic of modernity or postmodernity. Thus, for example, Raymond Williams in *Marxism and Literature* draws an insightful distinction between the "residual," the "dominant," and the "emergent."[29] This distinction is helpful in parsing the type of complex semantic field of action and reflection that anthropologists encounter, but Williams retains a narrative of progress by which one can only assume that once the emergent emerges it will become either dominant or subordinate and eventually residual. Alasdair Mac-Intyre, in his *Three Rival Versions of Moral Enquiry: Encyclopae-*

dia, Genealogy and Tradition, provides one of the richer and more charitable reading of each of these types in nineteenth-century thinking but is too readily satisfied with his own well-documented conclusion that there are logical incompatibilities of a formal sort that set these styles of reasoning apart. He does not inquire whether in a logic of practice the approaches are as totally separate and incompatible as he supposes or deduces.[30] Thus, these distinguished authors of quite different political stripes and a very few others who see the phenomenon all either seem to stumble on their unexamined belief in a progressive philosophy of history (however nuanced) or believe that the kind of internal rationalization process of doctrine that Max Weber described as a diacritic of a long-term trend contributing to modern formations must be respected, must be taken as the site of philosophic inquiry.

The even smaller set of thinkers who buck the despair and delegitimation of the contemporary tend to do so in the name of affirming earlier formations, before the fall. Thus, for example, Stephen Toulmin and Albert Jonsen in *The Abuse of Casuistry* make a strong case for a return to an approach to ethical problem-solving that preceded the nineteenth-century articulation of philosophy as the main competitor to theology for moral principles and systems. Although Toulmin and Jonsen provide a strong case and striking insights about the history of moral philosophy, one could argue that their categorical rejection of modern moral philosophy goes too far, especially as they themselves are concerned with medical ethics. Medical ethics, after all, is practiced in highly bureaucratized and rule-governed institutions that for legal and procedural reasons require some form of standard procedure. And that is not all bad. Medical ethics is the arena where the most detailed attention has been paid to the practice of ethical observation, judgment, and care. The attention to the singularity of cases and to the import of decision making as a process that draws on available resources is most richly explored in the literature on the "ethics of care." And as Michel Foucault began to show us, the whole range of issues of how an ethics of care and an imperative to know are today crying out for careful reexamination and a renewed curiosity as to how to invent pertinent forms and modes of practice.[31]

Fisher opened his book with a rhetorical question: "Could any pair of words seem as natural together as the words 'dispassionate knowledge'? Yet [ ] the passions were always understood to be essential for the search for knowledge."[32] They were indeed thought to be essential for a very long time, but the challenge was not so much whether the knower was gripped by vehement passions—that was basically a given—as how to find forms in which such passions could be made to make specific practices flourish, strengthen excellence or virtue. It is that challenge, as Max Weber and Michel Foucault (but also Aristotle, Nietzsche, McKeon, and Dewey) saw, that locates the problem of knowledge and ethics. Said another way, we are dealing here with the problematic relations of *anthropos, logos*, and *ethos*—and their saturation with diverse forms and figures of *pathos*. The multiple relations that have obtained, do obtain, and might obtain between these terms is the terrain to which the anthropologist of the contemporary is drawn. Consequently, because there is no outside to this terrain, it is one that anthropologists must seek to explore in terms of both how their own inquiry is organized, conducted, and circulated and, even more so, how it is being lived by those we choose to observe.

✸

MARKING TIME:
GERHARD RICHTER

Two Tasks: to defend the new against the old and to link
the old with the new.
> —Friedrich Nietzsche, 1873

Contemporary Modern

The natural world held a fascination for Paul Klee
throughout his life. "For the artist," he wrote, "dialogue
with nature remains a *conditio sine qua non*."[1] But what
kind of dialogue was the artist imagining? Klee specifies his vision in a letter to an art teacher in which he offered the following pedagogical advice: "Lead your students to nature, into nature! Let them experience how a bud develops, how a tree
grows, how a butterfly opens its wings so that they become as
prolific, as agile, as idiosyncratic as the great nature."[2] For Klee
this close observation and direct experience was not intended to
lead the student to a direct or literal imitation of nature's forms.
On the contrary, Klee conceived of the scrupulous observation
of nature as the precondition for the creation of previously
unseen and/or unknown forms. "Starting from nature," Klee
wrote, the students "will perhaps arrive at their own forms, and
one day be themselves nature, construct like nature."[3] By so

doing, one was essentially being true to nature. To participate in nature, or with nature, as it were, is continuously to create new forms; for this ceaseless process of creation and variation is precisely what happens in the natural world.

In a watercolor composed in 1930, entitled "Blossoms in the Night," Klee depicted what might be seen as a garden of flowers, painted in dark blue colors. All is clouded in an atmosphere of silence; all appears in place, wet and fleshy. None of the flowers represented are of similar shape. The flowers grow from all directions; the law of gravitation has momentarily been suspended, or so it seems. What the painting presents is not an imitation of existing flowers but flourishing vegetation that appears natural. What Klee paints are not actual but somehow plausible flowers. As a critic comments on a similar painting depicting strangely shaped fish: "[N]ames could come to mind that we would like to bestow upon these things, as analogies from biology rather than as designations."[4]

To explain the active relation of artistic creation and nature, Klee drew a distinction (in a 1912 article, *"Approches de l'art moderne"*) between impressionism and expressionism. The former adopts a passive attitude toward nature, stopping at the observation of form and sensory impact, thereby producing a certain immediacy of experience and affect. In contrast, expressionism introduces a temporal delay between experience and representation and thereby makes clear the absolute necessity for construction in art. By underscoring the necessity of construction, one claims a certain autonomy for art. Art's challenge is to rise "itself to the active construction of form."[5] Klee's interest lies not in a naïve or romantic depiction of nature—he is after all a modern artist—but in showing what nature might look like, as Klee said, once it *"has simply moved on just a little further than usual"* or perhaps, better, a nature peaceably askew, constructed differently, moving off orthogonally to the nature we know.[6]

Klee did not seek to venerate nature per se but to learn from nature its vital regularities, its formative processes. In a lecture given in 1924 he writes, "The artist does not accord to nature the same constraining importance that his numerous realist detractors do. The artist does not feel subjected, frozen forms do not represent to him the essence of the creative process in nature. Nature in process [*la nature naturante*] is more important to him than a state of nature [*la nature naturée*]."[7] Life forms could be otherwise. The past was different from the present; there is no scientific, ethical, or aesthetic reason that the future should not be different as well. Furthermore, no one knows what other forms exist in the universe in other galaxies, past, present, and future. Current conditions are merely a moment "fortuitously, accidentally stuck in space and time."[8] The challenge for the artist is to find a means to imitate the freedom found in natural processes, nature's motion, its variability, its unexpectedness. For Klee, then, there are two realms of creation and autonomy, art and nature; both are resplendent with possibilities in and of themselves, and for those capable of drawing the right analogies between them the varieties and variations of form appear without limit. It follows that a central challenge is to establish the right form of analogy. For Klee that form was neither metaphor nor metonym.

Biotechnical Forms

As early as 1929, a colleague of Klee's at the Bauhaus, Lazlo Moholy-Nagy, was speaking of "biotechnical forms" and proposing to put into practice a series of experiments that would improve organic form through mechanical perfection.[9] These projects were carried out during the (waning) days of modernism's heady optimism about its ability to shape the future. Moholoy-Nagy fully subscribed to a founding principle of the Bauhaus: bringing the sciences as well as the practical and the fine arts together into a common enterprise would produce an extraordinary synergy. Once the natural processes of transformation that permeated all living beings were understood and harnessed, they would be improved, thereby opening up radically new horizons, new modes of being, and new forms of life.

Still optimistic in 1937, after having fled Germany and come to the United States, Moholy-Nagy remained a modernist. Ever eager to write manifestos, he announced a program to "found a new science that will show how natural forms and schemas can be transposed without great difficulty into human production."[10] These developments point to a new twist in the older ideas of art as based in nature toward the modern idea of an artistic practice directed toward technique, a program of technique in which art and nature would be joined, improved, and made to serve humanity.

In 1934 the Museum of Modern Art in New York exhibited kitchen ware, household equipment, and other mass-produced objects. A year later, Alfred Barr curated the influential "Cubism and Abstract Art" exhibition at the museum, the "most elaborate, complex, [. . .] and the most bewildering exhibition arranged in the career of the Museum of Modern Art." In 1936 the museum invited the public to an exhibition of delphinium blooms. The press release announced a show of remarkable new varieties of delphinium developed through twenty-six years of cross-breeding and selection. Flower breeding had never before been officially confirmed by a major institution as a legitimate form of art. Flower breeder and photographer Edward Steichen proudly underscored his pleasure that "[B]y implication, flower breeding was recognized as one of the arts."[11] For Steichen this recognition was merited, given that his purpose in the breeding and in the exhibition was "to develop the ultimate aesthetic possibilities of the delphinium."[12] If objects of ordinary life were appropriately displayed, why not modified nature?

During eight days, between 500 and 1,000 Steichen delphinium stalks were put on display in the ground floor of the museum. At the time, Steichen was known as a photographer; he acted as chair of the museum's Advisory Committee on Photography. Comparing flower breeding to the traditional means of art, Steichen remarked that instead of

> [w]ords or pigment or tone, the plant breeder works and struggles with factors and forces that have been locked up within the various species of plants he may employ for tens of thousands of years. The very process of breaking up long closely inbred habits opens up the gates that release new forms, patterns, and colors. [. . .] The delphinium and many of our garden flowers still have unexplored potentialities awaiting development that will bring us flowers beyond any of our present concepts or imaginings.[13]

Struggling with the factors and forces of nature, Steichen received unexpected aid from the pharmaceutical industry. It was in the early 1930s that geneticists found that they were able to double the chromosome count in plants by means of the drug colchicines. Coincidentally, Steichen himself was taking the drug for his gout. With the help of colchicines, Steichen "forced strains of heredity to improbable outcomes. In a few hours, mutations of plant material were produced that might not occur in nature in a thousand years."[14] Manipulating the factor of mutation, Steichen enhanced breeding's creative potential, producing flowers in the most astonishing colors, offering an undeniable appeal to the public.

Household objects, flowers, and an undeniable appeal to the public. How banal. But how should one take up the banal? How should one take up living material? These questions would haunt artists, critics, scientists, politicians, and the proverbial average citizen throughout the twentieth century.

Richter: Double Negations

I do not wish to imitate a photograph, I want to make one.

Photographs are almost nature.[15]

The painting of the German artist Gerhard Richter (b. 1931) is compelling for its striking visual qualities, perpetually renewed formal experimentation, and conceptual challenges. Richter's work has spanned an impressive variety of forms that would be difficult to gather convincingly under one stylistic label. Richter belongs to no school yet is conversant with (and appears to be an imagistic commentary on) much of contemporary art as well as the history of Western painting. Not only are Richter's images stimulating and frequently pleasurable to look at, they are also challenging to think about, in part because they are so hard to classify or interpret.

Art Critics and Others

As a series of commentators have discovered (and demonstrated by their mutually contradictory views), providing an incisive and convincing interpretation of Richter's work is a problematic task. The challenge of naming, interpreting, and criticizing what Richter is doing and has produced is vexing, particularly for the few indefatigably confident critics to whom Richter has afforded repeated access over the years, only to repudiate their attempts to explain his intentions and stymie their interpretation of his work.[16] Undaunted by Richter's half-exasperated, half-amused disclaimers, critics such as Benjamin Buchloh continue to stride confidently through the critical landscape, searching for the correct ideological umbrella while Richter rains ever more heavily on the interpretive parade. And this practice of complicity and distance has gone on for decades.

Richter writes little but frequently uses the interview as a means to stay in the public light. From his earliest experiences with critics and journalists, Richter had performed a studied reluctance to commit himself and a stylized naïveté about the meaning of his practice. In sum, the interviews are a form he has learned to use both to engage the attention of the critical industry and to disabuse—while staying connected with—those on whom he is no doubt dependent for publicity, production of sophisticated attention, and the like. He skirts their pretensions even while he baits them to try harder. Here is one example:

> **RS.** The [third] explanation for erasing or paring down an image is that what you are left with in the end is something irreducible or basic. Rather than performing a symbolic act of destruction or painting loss, you arrive at a distillation of the image's essential qualities.
> **GR.** I hope that's the case. You can say that. I can't.
> **RS.** But if that is the purpose of working in this way then what you finally have is neither the depicted object in itself nor a clear mirror image of the subject struggling to perceive that object, but a strange in-between entity representing the exchange of appearance between the object painted and the subject looking at it, the thing and the viewer.
> **GR.** That is something for intellectuals. (*laughter*)[17]

Thus, as opposed to Michel Foucault or Gilles Deleuze, for Richter interviews do not provide a space in which to try out preliminary ideas or discard older ones. After all, he is not a philosopher but a painter. This claim, of course, does not mean that Richter is not thinking. However, as Gilles Deleuze correctly asserts, painting is not about opinion, or about the artist's beliefs, or about concepts.[18] Finally, Richter is not a painter of ideas, despite what certain critics maintain. Gerhard Richter is a painter of images. He makes images of contemporary life insofar as the contemporary world's vast repertoire of images can be painted.[19] Consequently, what Richter has to contribute to thinking must be found in his image production, not in his words.

Our Contemporary

If modernism was characterized by an insistent search for the shock of the new, the contemporary ethos seeks neither to shock for its own sake nor doctrinally to eradicate historical reference. Equally, aware of its historical moment, the contemporary artist does not repudiate shock or historical erasure in an outright or aprioristic manner. Rather, a practitioner taking up a contemporary stance is perplexed about how to treat representation, affect, and reference. Consistently, that perplexity extends to what to do with the by now historical doctrines of modernism or to those of countermodernisms. Critics have applied the label of "antinostalgic romantic" to Richter, but the term "romantic" carries such heavy semantic and political baggage that I prefer simply to call him "a painter of the contemporary world."

As Richter said in 1983:

> Traditional, supposedly old works of art are not old but contemporary. [ ] Their permanent presence compels us to produce something different, which is neither better nor worse, but which has to be different because we painted the Isenheim Altar yesterday. [ ] But the better we know tradition—i.e., ourselves—and the more responsibly we deal with it, the better things we shall make similar, and the better things we shall make different.[20]

Despite the mutually contradictory views of Richter's work— romantic and not romantic, politically conservative or ethically advanced, reactionary, postmodern, or contemporary—and its own changeable styles (from landscapes of a sort to abstractions of another sort, from the use of gray monochromes to vibrant, "acidlike" palettes, from intimate portraits of private domains to visual evocations of murderers and military destruction), there is a critical consensus, shared and encouraged by the artist himself, that two topics central to Richter's works are photography and nature. Throughout his long and prolific career, Richter has consistently (although not uniquely) used the banal photographic image as a take-off point for many of his works, including at least some of the vast number of abstract paintings (all called "abstract painting"—*Abstraktes Bild*—plus a number). Peter Osborne, the critic whose work has most guided me, makes a convincing case that rather than translating *"Bild"* as "painting," it would be more accurate to say "image."[21]

Although less insistently present thematically, Richter has intermittently returned to evocations of or allusions to "nature," in diverse series of apparent landscapes or seeming portrayals of sea, sky, ice, waterways, crests, or meadows, which span his decades of painting. Upon closer inspection, however, Richter's portrayals of natural things are enigmatic in that they are never what they appear to be at first glance, in terms of either technique or subject matter.

And yet . . . and yet.

Nature

One of the topics on which Richter has pronounced with force and extravagant bluntness is "nature." The following position statements are from a 1986 interview.

> Every beauty that we see in landscape—every enchanting color effect, or tranquil scene, or powerful atmosphere, every gentle linearity or magnificent spatial depth or whatever—is our projection; and we can switch it off at a moment's notice, to reveal only the appalling horror and ugliness.

109

Nature is so inhuman that it is not even criminal. It is every-thing that we must basically overcome and reject—because, for all our own superabundant horrendousness, cruelty and vile-ness, we are still capable of producing a spark of hope, which is coeval with us, and which we can also call love (this has noth-ing to do with unconscious, bestial, mammalian nurturing be-havior). Nature has none of this. Its stupidity is absolute.

Of course, my landscapes are not only beautiful or nostalgic, with a Romantic or classical suggestion of lost Paradise, but above all "untruthful" (even if I didn't always find a way of showing it); and by "untruthful" I mean the glorifying way we look at Nature—Nature, which in all its forms is always against us, because it knows no meaning, no pity, no sympathy, be-cause it knows nothing and is absolutely mindless: the total an-tithesis of ourselves, absolutely inhuman.[22]

Hearing these remarks, it would seem that Richter is the ulti-mate counterromantic. As one critic has aptly observed: "The execration of nature matches the intensity of romantic hymns of adoration."[23] Yet, Richter's pronouncements are so absolute, so universal, and so strident that they are unlikely to be completely tenable, stable, or sincere. In fact, there is here a tension, to which I will return below, that characterizes Richter's work more generally: his struggles with a space of complex double negation.

Nuancing the absolutism, another critic perceptively writes that Richter has an urban attitude toward nature insofar as he approaches it "as a collection of images or *tableaux*." The city dweller's regret at the loss of nature's immediacy and comfort, to the extent that it is still felt, is countered by what Rilke at the beginning of the twentieth century wished to recognize as a beneficial side to this distancing, even going so far as to call it "a liberating parable for our destiny."[24] For Richter, then, nature is present, but it is neither a home nor a source of meaning nor an origin point. It is obviously neither sacred nor inviolable, whatever such terms could mean to a contemporary artist in the twenty-first century. Today we are obliged to establish a relationship with what others, for example Paul Klee, with seeming ease, have called nature. It follows that establishing such a relationship, or even identifying the elements that might go into such an imagined connection (or disconnection), is not a given but a problem.

As early as 1962, Richter wrote, "the idea that art copies nature is a fatal misconception. Art has always operated against nature and for reason."[25] Whatever Richter may mean by "reason," he certainly does not mean an ideology or a program or an idea. He emphatically underscores this point in his contemptuous dismissal of those artists who take an idea as their point of departure for their work—"that's illustration." Rather, Richter wants to begin painting—he has frequently remarked at the difficulty of beginning—as a search for form.

> This reflects my conviction that form, the cohesion of formal elements, the structure of the phenomenal appearance of matter (= form), generates a content—and that I can manipulate the outward appearance as it comes, in such a way as to yield this or that content. [ ] I have only to act in accordance with the laws and conditions of form in order to get the materialization right. (127)

This claim sounds like a return to form inherent in matter itself. And, rather surprisingly, he does return to nature as a touchstone and confirmation.

> It also conforms to a general principle of Nature; for Nature, too, does not develop an organism in accordance with an idea: Nature lets its forms and modifications come, within the framework of its given facts and with the help of chance. And this theory is no less useless than ludicrous if I paint bad pictures. (128–29)

111

Upon reflection, the return to nature is less surprising as it too completes another turn of a double negation without resolution. Painting is radically different from nature; painting is like nature. Painting and nature negate each other. Or almost.

In this light, Richter's Delphic proclamation—"I do not wish to imitate a photograph, I want to make one"—begins to make sense.[26] Especially in the light of another of his maxims: "Photographs are almost nature."[27] Or better yet, perhaps he means that today nature can be approached almost like photographs can be approached—as a first-order given, but not as a transparent source of meaning. Photography and nature are facets of an image-space and the material of the artist's problem. And part of his work.

Photography

The second topic, then, is photography. For Richter, almost from the beginning of his career, the photographic image has been a fundamental starting point, a confrontation with the modern world's primary materiality. As a critic tellingly observes, Richter tenaciously adhered to a primacy of images as a means to redefine the practice of pictorial production. "To create a painting is to fulfill something seen in the secondary reality of the painted image. The initial reality, the model, is no longer a motif *à la Cézanne*, but a photograph, that is to say, already an image."[28] For decades Richter has been an avid, almost obsessive, collector and archivist of ordinary photographs, that is to say, family photographs, those from the popular press, and the like. He refers to these images as "banal," adding emphatically, with a reference to the "banality of evil," that "banality means a little bit more than unimportant."[29] Critics have constructed much social commentary on the banality of the contemporary world *tout court* into his work. Richter, once again, enters into

discussions in interviews and then, faced with these constructions, distances himself from such definitive interpretations.

Reflecting on Richter's use of photographic images as given
matter, a critic captures a distinctive aspect of Richter's relation
to the reservoir of photographic images: "The amateur is usually understood to be someone who is either unwilling or un-
able to achieve mastery of a profession, but in photography the
situation is reversed: the amateur is the precondition for the professional because he is closer to the [ ] 'that has been' of photography."[30] As is well known (massively documented and reflected upon), there have been tensions and complex relations
between painting and photography ever since the appearance of
the technique during the mid-nineteenth century. Further, and
this is equally pertinent, there has been within photographic
practice itself a tradition of marking a distinction between the
amateur and the professional. The professional photographer
is challenged to establish the distinction of her work either
through a claim to be a master of technique or as a maker of self-
consciously artistic visual effects and affects. These references
have been, often if not exclusively, references to painting. In fact,
the distinction between amateur and professional has been a diacritic of the myriad modernist approaches to photography, ex-
ploring and exploiting multiple manners of creating art and
thereby distinguishing the products from those of the presumed
facility of ordinary photographic representation.

This route of the traditional modernist distinction is not the
one Richter has followed, at least not in its standard manner. In
fact, his relationship to art photography remains unspecified; he
seems not to take it explicitly into consideration. It has simply
not been an object of his concern. And one can see why: he is
doing something else. He has sought to invent an orthogonal
relation—proximate, distant, oblique, in a word, adjacent—to
the problem, to the dilemma of high and low, representation
and art. To make this claim is to say neither that he has resolved

the dilemma nor that he has succeeded in dissolving it or over-coming it. The dilemma remains present and unresolved, but Richter takes it up differently.

Unpacking what Richter is doing (and has been doing for decades) requires the introduction of a series of further distinc-tions. Of course, many artists (Andy Warhol, Roy Lichtenstein, and Robert Rauschenberg among many others) have turned to photographs or images drawn from other mass media such as comics or movies and used them in their work. The secondary literature explores Richter's connections and disjunctions from and with these artists and the movements associated with them. It is striking to an outsider how concerned these critics are with classifying styles and with identifying influences. As one would expect, Richter situates himself as both proximate to and distant from his contemporaries. Thus, on the one hand, Richter ac-knowledges his debt to Warhol and his use of photographic im-agery in all its banality:

> I believe that the quintessential task of every painter in any time has been to concentrate on the essential. The hyper-realists didn't do that, they painted everything, every detail. That's why they were such a surprise. But for me it was obvi-ous that I had to wipe out the details. I was happy to have a method that was rather mechanical. In that regard I owe some-thing to Warhol. He legitimized the mechanical. He showed me how it is done. It is a normal state or working to eliminate things. But Warhol showed me this modern way of letting de-tails disappear, or at least he validated its possibilities. He did it with silkscreening and photography, and I did it through mechanical wiping. It was a very liberating act.[31]

Richter's approach differs from that of Warhol, who increasingly made the use of restylized photographic imagery his signature, his brand. Richter, in contrast, aims to desubjectivize his own presence. And this stylistic inconsistency, this refusal of painterly dogma, marks Richter as a contemporary image maker and experimentalist rather than a builder of programs or theories.[32] Nor has he been drawn to the persona of the artist as the site of artistic creation or genius or even practice in an exalted sense (for example, Jackson Pollack). "Photography," writes Richter, "keeps you from stylizing, from seeing 'falsely' from giving an overly personal interpretation to the subject."[33] Richter, one can say, presents keen views of a world of images, but, unlike Warhol, he does not yield to a worldview. That being said, Richter has posed willingly for scores of photographs in his studio.

Given the type of objects he works over, and given his stance toward them, Richter's experiments begin with a double conditioning. There are a number of aspects to this approach. Primary among them is the place of temporality or historicity. Taking mediated images as the primary material implies beginning with a certain mode of temporality already as an inherent part of the object to be reworked. "Every photograph," Barthes has argued, is "a certificate of presence": the presence of the past within the present. The banal image, however, itself carries with it a range of further possibilities and connotations beyond those Barthes is concerned with:

> Like the *chronicle*, photographic recording can participate in the writing of present history, to the extent that it shows the present as it will be understood later ("this will have been"). So doing, photography situates itself between historical action (as always more-or-less blind involvement in the present) and the retrospective interpretation of that action. But at the same time it can also constitute an anticipated nostalgia, a manner of projecting a nostalgic interpretation onto the present, and thus transforming it systematically into the past.[34]

This tendency of the ordinary photograph to incline toward nostalgia, sentimentality, trivia, and so on can itself be taken up in many ways. One is to situate it as a kind of unexceptional first-order consciousness of the kind Pierre Bourdieu has ascribed to the snapshot. Another is the fascistic or totalitarian uses that such sentimentality can lend itself to, a theme Richter returns to frequently. Richter is aware of these risks, in part because his critics accuse him of sometimes not being sufficiently vigilant about his own use of images of dubious political standing. He is quick to point out that one must avoid confusing the content—of a Nazi uncle, of the corpses of the Baader-Meinhof group, of famous white men, of bombers—and his image making.

Whatever political or ethical judgments one might make of Richter's "message," the fundamental error to avoid is to take it up as if it were an unmediated form, a photograph.

> Whether dealing with media-based material or some type of message, whether stemming from the everyday or the artistic, what characterizes all Richter's motifs and pretexts is that they are treated at the same time as exemplary of a genre in which the consciousness of their mediated nature is still absent. It is the painter who makes them exemplary or transforms them into characteristic representations of way of representing and signifying.[35]

In sum, Richter's use of photographic images enables him to use the objectivity or givenness of the photographic image to counter subjectivist tendencies in painting. The image helps set both the apparent content of the painting as well as its composition. It also sets a historical frame, although the contemporary use of that framing remains open.

Marking Time

There is another dimension of temporality in Richter's work: its historical reference to modernism. Richter is a secessionist and not a revolutionary. He takes his distance from Duchamp's ready-made, upon which and through which he renounced painting out of loyalty to it. Although Duchamp's swerve was itself secessionist (as Thierry de Duve has demonstrated), it was an extravagant avant-gardist gesture with enormous consequences for artistic practice. Richter differs from Duchamp especially in his relation to the historicity of the image on both a first- and second-order level. Richter's secession from avant-gardism and its revolutionary aspirations and pretensions as well as his ardent disdain for its strictures allow him to broaden his repertoire of images, techniques, and thoughts. Could that be what he means by "reason"?

> It seems to me that the invention of the Readymade was the invention of reality. It was the crucial discovery that what counts is reality, not any world-view whatever. Since then, painting has never represented reality; it has been reality (creating itself). And sooner or later the value of this reality will have to be denied, in order (as usual) to set up pictures of a better world.[36]

While learning from Duchamp—Richter has produced mirrors and other such objects that are clear reworkings of Duchamp—and those that followed him, by eschewing worldviews and a linear approach to artistic change, Richter is freed to reach back to earlier generations of painters who struggled to position painting within a context marked by the emergence of photography. Richter can learn from Monet, Delacroix, or even Cézanne without having to imitate them or obliterate their memory. As the "idea of modernism" as a utopian project, in T. J. Clark's rendering, has failed, an analogous but hardly identical encounter with the archive of image making can be taken up once again, but differently.[37] The image is once again, as it has been many times, not only the problem but the means to confront the multifaceted site of problematization. Of course, confrontation, as Osborne points out, does not mean success. And here, image making departs from science, in that its criteria of success are unknown and unstable.

If Barthes is right that photography, even the most banal, is a medium that brings forth a *"punctum,"* a decisive moment of time, Richter takes this process one step further into historicity. Again, Richter generally works with the photograph. By so doing, his image-altering, image-making practices produce a historical consciousness of the photograph and its contents as well as the concept of image making itself. Every photo-painting may well be a certificate of presence, but it is also a certificate of history, or better, historicity. As Osborne writes,

> Photo-painting is one way of painting after the readymade that incorporates a consciousness of the crisis of painting into its constitutive procedures—procedures which, while they may be tied to the history of the craft through technique, derive both their extrinsic rationale and intrinsic logic from their critical reflection on the concept of painting itself.[38]

This practice achieves a "double-distanced reference to the object."[39] But not an obliteration of painting as a practice.

> Double negation: the negative dialectics in which the second negation, rather than either returning us to our starting point or reconstituting the identity of each term from the standpoint of a new, "higher" positivity, *marks time*, dwells on the reciprocal negativity of the nonidentity of the two terms, and finds there, within the determinacy of their mutual negation, the utopian shadow of the reconciliation it is denied.[40]

On this insightful reading, Richter's paintings are "negatives"; negatives of paintings, negatives of photographs. The negation of painting by photography by painting and vice versa is not an elimination of either. Rather, it is "a kind of stalemate. That points beyond itself only negatively."[41] It is a historical image space whose transformation has been long in coming. Here is another moment of proximity and distance: to photography, its temporality, and the historicity of representation that it embodies. Osborne is right, Richter's work marks time or perhaps temporality or even historicity. Perhaps even more startlingly, it marks all three at the same time.[42]

Abstract Images

All of this conceptual work (as well as all of the image making to the degree that it can be said to be dependent on the conceptual work or at least not in total disjunction from it) is dependent on the historical ontology of the photograph. The double negation could also be described as a dilemma. In logic a dilemma is a situation in which there are two incompatible principles. Since they are incompatible, any movement forward based on them leads to difficulties. In logic the only way to resolve a dilemma is to change one of the starting points. Artistic practice of course is not logic, and consequently an unresolved and even irresolvable dilemma can be the source and the medium of a productive and dynamic tension. Motion is not resolution, if by that one means overcoming. If one of those poles begins to shift, the tension that constitutes the dilemma slackens. Hence, what if the century and a half of solidity of the photograph as the baseline representational tool began to change? What would happen to this "negative" work? What would contemporary images look like then?

Gerhard Richter has painted abstract paintings for a very long time, although one should add that diverse techniques are covered under that label.[43] They gained increasing prominence both for the artist and for his critics, however, as the decades of the 1980s and 1990s moved along. How should one think about Richter's relation to a tradition of abstract painting that existed decades before he began his own unlimited series of *Abstrakten Bilder?*

Richter was never drawn to the purist, avant-gardist gestures of high modernism or its utopian programs. As with the romanticism of the romantics, so, too, with the purity of the abstract expressionists and its heroization of the artistic gesture, Richter was perfectly willing to work with the images produced but to strip them of the affect formerly attached to them. Robert Storr quotes Richter in conversation with Buchloh as describing his abstract images as "An assault on the falsity and religiosity of the way people glorified abstraction, with such phony reverence."[44] Here as elsewhere, Richter is analytic and caustic, showing that images and affect or technique that had been bundled together could be broken down and separated without loss. Repetition in art was usually a betrayal.

In any case, the situation in which abstract expressionism, pop art, and their successors emerged has once again changed. "By the late 1960s, however, the 'golden age' of abstract expressionism has disappeared through a combination of developments within art itself (the theoretical implosion of the putative aesthetic autonomy of cultural modernism) and changes within wider society (the appropriation of the avant-garde by the art market and the culture industry)."[45] To say that such trends have continued would be to restate the blatantly obvious. And hence, among other consequences, we should not be surprised at the proliferation of debates about the "end of art."[46] And yet, fortunately, people keep painting—and making images.

The critical appreciation of Richter's abstractions is surprisingly tentative. There has been a rather informal inventory of technique and a more systematic archiving in a *Catalogue Raisonné.*[47] But the critic's conceptual work has lagged behind that of the artist. Osborne offers the most astute openings for such an analytic, but, as he acknowledges, the analysis is only in its early stages.

In closing, for I am trying to go elsewhere, let us turn to that preliminary effort and comprehension at identifying significance, as Max Weber would say. Osborne notes that the status of the photograph is changing as digital photography and digital video become increasingly a part of the image-scape. The question is whether or not digital techniques, technology, and practice are transforming the concept of the image in essential ways. For my purpose, what is most relevant about this unfolding and unpredictable process is that it is making the historicity of photographic technology more and more evident, more and more visible. Osborne convincingly argues that we are beginning to see "The illusion of absolute analogy carried by the epistemically privileged form of the image in general, to which all other forms of image production had progressively to accommodate themselves in order to produce a credible denotative effect."[48] The historical disassembling of technique, technology, and practice produces a marking of their historicity and opens a space for new concepts and new practices to emerge.

To condense a complicated, heterogeneous, and fluid set of developments into a synecdochic example, now that PhotoShop and other such programs are commercialized and black-boxed, visual effects such as Richter's use of blurring or moiré (and related techniques) are a standardized quality of the contemporary image. Of course that does not mean that their aesthetic or conceptual use is simply given or critically worthless, but it does mean that they no longer inherently play a role in negation. They are no longer challenging or a priori disconcerting. Along with the long list of PhotoShop options, they are now simply an available technique, ready for use. One is reminded here of Duchamp's affirmation of the tube of paint, the emergence of which as an industrial and commercial product undermined and demystified the tacit craft practice of making colors. Its standardization produced mourning, nostalgia, and regret for awhile, but obviously the tube of paint did not mean the end of artistic work. Quite the contrary.

What happens to painterly image making once PhotoShop is available online at Amazon.com? What happens to image making once the site of the negative has shifted both technically and conceptually (if it has)? How does one mark time under such conditions? What is the material to be worked on, the bearer of sensation, and affect, in the contemporary world? Questions, no doubt, for the critic to pose and reflect on; and for the maker of images to work through, if he can figure out how to do so.

Remediation

The elements of a concise, systematic, and appropriately tentative overview of the status of images in the twenty-first century are articulated in Lev Manovich's *The Language of the New Media*.[49] His analysis turns to the history of avant-garde cinema as the paradigmatic form of image making (and narration) in the twentieth century, and how computers (and their associated practices and practitioners) have made it possible both to continue the techniques of cinema as well as to transform them radically. It is in that nexus of partial continuity and partial change that he situates what he calls, with a certain appropriate hesitation, "the language of the new media." The hesitation comes from his appreciation that "language" is a misleading term to characterize the forms under consideration and can serve only as a placeholder. It would be better to describe this nexus of elements, procedures, connections, capacities, and limitations as the "logic" and "economy," that is to say, the rationality, of the new media.[50] The categories of the new media are useful in comprehending the types, components, and stylizations of objects in the image world at the beginning of the twenty-first century. In that light, they can provide a transition from the reflections on Richter's artistic work and its problem-space into a more general perspective on contemporary techno-objects.

Manovich chooses the Soviet film maker Dziga Vertov's 1929 *Man with a Movie Camera* as the iconic starting point for the aesthetic modernity as well as avant-garde desires of cinema. Along with many other cinema and media critics and historians, Manovich argues for this film as marking a significant cultural threshold that opened a problem space for invention and discovery that (perhaps) has only recently been (partially) surpassed. *The Language of New Media* crisply analyzes the ways in which avant-garde techniques in cinema (and related media) are now becoming generalized into a set of techniques and procedures that can be applied to the manipulation of all cultural production, thanks to the dissemination of the (ever more powerful) computer. That being said, the question of the specificity of visual objects remains: one must be wary of the epochal enthusiasms and overgeneralizations. Here the task is to select a few specific dimensions of Manovich's panorama so as to provide analytic help relevant to the task at hand: an eventual analysis of new objects in the biological sciences and their effectuations and countereffectuations with *anthropos*.

The analysis of new media might provide aid in fashioning tools to approach new developments in the biosciences such as synthetic biology, or in other scientific and/or engineering domains such as nano-technology. Obviously neither synthetic biology nor nano-technology can be directly equated to either contemporary painting or new media. And yet, computers, databases, manipulability, variations, and other such techniques and practices are used in many current relevant domains, especially but not uniquely bio-informatics. It is an empirical question as to how software, for example, is used to construct new objects both in the strictly technical sense as well as in the *habitus* of a generation of practitioners who grew up with video

123

games and a comfort with programming. The algorithms, languages, infrastructure, styles, and games of the new media are increasingly part of the ethos of the practitioners of all high-tech fields as well as artistic ones. The approach taken here, however, does not depend on either direct identity or analogy between domains, although there can be specific identity of tools; the application of abstract questions in the creation of software is often equally salient in the work of artists and biologists.

Objects

The dimension of the new media most relevant to these scientific and engineering fields is its reconstruction of the object. The term "object" is useful for a number of reasons. To begin with, it establishes a basis for making links to other significant twentieth-century projects (artistic, scientific, technological, political, ethical, and the like). Thus, for example, during the 1920s the term "object" was substituted for "work of art" in a number of different sites ranging from the Russian constructivists and productivists who sought to make their work an integrated part of a larger project of social revolution and transformation of modes of living. Or the Bauhaus, arguably the most notable of the projects attempting to bring industrial design into an overt interdependency with art, craft, industry, and daily life. Each of these projects, whether reformist or revolutionary, in their innumerable varieties, sought to overcome the focus on singular works of art through constructing carefully (attention to use and style) and thoughtfully (conceptually mediated) objects designed to be available for standardized uses in the daily life of industrial societies. The goal of the Bauhaus was to subject the production of objects to criteria of mass production and broad utility rather than uniqueness and aesthetic refinement as ends in-and-of-themselves.

Members of the Bauhaus (and related enterprises) began with the problem of how to reshape daily life in industrial society through the transformation of their own creative practice. To achieve this goal, Bauhaus workshops began with the assumption that the individual artist or craftsperson would have to learn to work with others within an orchestrated division of labor and to produce objects that would be disseminated on a mass scale (or at a significantly greater scale than previously was the case). Determining how to do this took years of experimentation and work. Eventually some fruits of these experimental labors were disembedded from their original sites in accord with the original project. Reformers at the Bauhaus like Walter Gropius, or those more politically radical like his successor Hannes Meyer, agreed on the necessity for the transfer to industry and into society as an important if not unique criterion of success. While the aesthetic value of an object was not equated with its acceptance by the market, its failure was no longer a mark of its distinction either. Granted that they differed on how they thought the relations (and ends) of industry and society should be configured ultimately.

Broadly speaking, during the last decade of the nineteenth century and the first of the twentieth century, the fine arts (and crafts) continued to pursue an artisan model of artistic creation with its commitment to the existence of the specially endowed individual creator. It was only in the 1910s—when some artists began to assemble collages and montages from already existing cultural "parts"—that aspects of the emerging industrial method of production entered the realm of the arts and crafts. For the visual media, photomontage was the breakthrough expression of this approach; by the early 1920s, photomontage was a common practice.[51] Its links to cinema and advertising are to be noted; the latter was present at the Bauhaus in each of its stages. In other domains of practice, lineages and dating would vary somewhat—for example, in architecture the chronology of emergence of the program is somewhat earlier—but the basic point remains valid.

Paul Klee's artistic production, for example, rests on a belief in the existence of basic design elements that can be identified and made systematic. Chris Kelty observes:

> The systematization of aesthetic design elements, and of practices for producing them, is the salient comparative point because it is these design elements that have systematically been refined and incorporated into, for example, Photoshop or Final Cut Pro—giving them the appearance of being mere transparent tools for the creation of new objects, instead of what they are: accretions of previous aesthetic, scientific, algorithmic, and practical concerns coalesced into a tool: "Bezier curve" or "jump cut."[52]

Experimentation with combinatorial possibilities mean that individual objects were frequently set within a series of controlled variations. Klee's teaching at the Bauhaus, as that of his colleagues, sought to identify, codify, and teach these principles. The curriculum in the later years of the Bauhaus centered on the exploration of primary forms and colors, their recombination in a systematic fashion, and a reflective analysis of form and type.[53] This schema applied to painting as well as weaving, architecture as well as metallurgy. Of course, many at the Bauhaus (and elsewhere) continued to produce singular works of art.

Neither the Soviet experiments nor the Bauhaus successfully worked out a stable relationship to the larger political forces in Europe during the 1920s and 1930s. The Soviet state as well as the Nazis dissolved these experimental sites, denouncing them as decadent and contrary to the true destiny of history and the people. It is worth remembering that not only the Soviet leaders in the early 1920s but even some Nazis were in favor of modernist reform (until 1933). And throughout the interwar years, Soviets, National Socialists, and liberals all agreed on the need for standardization, efficiency, and the transformation of daily life even if they disagreed on methods and visions. Many of the types, forms, elements, practices, work regimens, and objects experimented with in the interwar period survived and returned during and after World War II in altered political and social settings. To an extraordinary degree, the objects (housing, furniture, textiles, utensils, advertising, print, etc.) created in these experimental sites are still with us.

Remediation

By the early 1980s, cultural production as the site of postmodernism in the strict sense of "after modernism" was moving away from the core guiding principles of avant-garde modernism. For example, the near sacrality of the materials (language, colors, sounds, body movements, etc.) themselves as the essential ground no longer held sway. The imperative to "make it new" was changing its meaning. In its place, the norm was becoming "endless recycling and quoting of past media content, aesthetic sensibilities, and historical forms, from an ever-widening archive, so as to produce new 'international styles.'"[54] These styles are volatile and often hard to distinguish from fashion. Although the practice of putting together a media object from already existing, commercially distributed elements existed from the early days of modernist media (e.g., photomontage, assemblage), new media technology further standardized the practice and made it vastly easier to perform. Contemporary media objects "are rarely created completely from scratch; usually they are assembled from ready-made parts."[55] But the use of ready-made parts no longer has any primary shock value. It takes a lot more today to *épater les bourgeois*; avant-gardism has to compete with other stylizations of the new and the contemporary.

Two media theorists propose the term "remediation" as a

cover term for the work of contemporary media. For them, "re-mediation" consists in combinations of "translating, refashioning, and reforming other media, both on the level of content and form."[56] One significant consequence of the modularity, variations, and remediations of objects has been the creation of ever-expanding databases. New enterprises have flourished to provide selection services to rapidly identify sought-after objects from this extravagant availability. The scale is global. Selection, access, remediation, reuse, reconfiguration, are the challenge and the source of value.

There is a second connotation to the term, however: improvement. This connotation is a secondary one for media practitioners, but for the new scientific disciplines like synthetic biology or nano-technology it is vitally relevant. The promise (hyped and not, potential and virtual) of instrumental results has shaped the life sciences over the last several decades; the promise of miracles of medical cures, environmental amelioration, enhanced experience, and their ilk continue to drive the funding from government, industry, and venture capital as well as the projects themselves. Today, while these vectors continue to power direction and decision making, a dimension that is gaining greater significance is a shift to refashioning, recomposing, and remediating objects taken to be the products of evolution. Hence we are faced with the question: As previously with the objects of history and art, so too with evolution?

✴

NOTES

PREFACE

1. Rabinow, P. 2003. *Anthropos Today: Reflections on Modern Equipment*. Princeton: Princeton University Press.

2. Rabinow, P., and T. Dan-Cohen. 2006. *A Machine to Make a Future: Biotech Chronicles*. 2nd edition. Princeton: Princeton University Press.

3. Collier, S. J., A. Lakoff, and P. Rabinow. 2004. "Biosecurity: Towards an Anthropology of the Contemporary." *Anthropology Today* 20:3–7. For more details, see www.anthropos-lab.net.

4. For more details, see www.synberc.org.

5. Pauly, P. 1987. *Controlling Life: Jacques Loeb and the Engineering Ideal in Biology*. Oxford: Oxford University Press.

INTRODUCTION

1. Definitions from the online Windows dictionary.

2. Rabinow, P. 1975. *Symbolic Domination: Cultural Form and Historical Change in Morocco*. Chicago: University of Chicago Press.

3. Williams, R. 1977. *Marxism and Literature*. Oxford: Oxford University Press, pp. 121–27.

4. Rabinow, *Anthropos Today*.

5. Ibid.; Rabinow, P. 1996. *Making PCR: A Story of Biotechnology*. Chicago: University of Chicago Press; Rabinow, P. 1999. *French DNA: Trouble in Purgatory*. Chicago: University of Chicago Press. Rabinow and Dan-Cohen, *A Machine to Make a Future*.

6. On nonmetric space, see Delanda, M. 2004. *Intensive Science and Virtual Philosophy*. London: Continuum.

7. For more details, see www.anthropos-lab.net.

8. Dewey, J. 1991. *Logic: The Theory of Inquiry*. Vol. 12. *The Later Works, 1925–38*. Carbondale: Southern Illinois Press.

9. For example: "the way of reconstruction is not through giving at-

tention to form at the expense of substantial content, as is the case with techniques that are used only to develop and refine still more purely formal skills." Dewey, J. 1948. *Reconstruction in Philosophy*. Boston: Beacon Press, p. vi.

10. Ryan, A. 1995. *John Dewey and the High Tide of American Liberalism*. New York: Norton, 28, quoting "From Absolutism to Experimentalism," in *Later Works*, vol. 5, p. 155. One explanation of this disconnect between form and content is provided by Alan Ryan in his biography of Dewey. Ryan also quotes Dewey from his essay "From Absolutism to Experimentalism": "'Upon the whole, the forces that have influenced me have come from persons and from situations more than from books . . .' but Dewey was a shy man who disapproved of personalities, and in everything but his shortest polemical essays he disguised all too effectively what situations and persons they were." Perhaps a simpler explanation of this contradiction is rhetorical: to move professional philosophers in the twentieth century, one had to talk to them in their own jargon; if one was to engage their attention at all, one had to operate in a discursive space located adjacent to their highly disciplined discourse and its tight genre constraints. As the aim here, however, is not to build a new system (nor to influence analytic philosophers) but rather to continue to assemble a tool kit of concepts, we are justified in taking helpful ideas, procedures, and concepts from Dewey and moving on. Among the historical insights gleaned one would include the observation that while authorized practitioners of philosophy in the twentieth century articulated the necessity of inquiry into the present, major figures such as Dewey or Wittgenstein or Heidegger or Rorty were unwilling to practice, or perhaps simply incapable of practicing, what they advocated. The proclamation of the end of traditional philosophy remained the last bastion of traditional philosophers. We would have to wait for Michel Foucault (or Gilles Deleuze) to see what such an enterprise—thinking about and within actuality—might look like.

11. Thanks to James Faubion for his enlightenment on this issue.

12. Dewey, *Logic*, pp. 345–46.

"Inquiry begins in an *indeterminate* situation, and not only begins in it but is controlled by its specific qualitative nature. Inquiry, as the set of operations by which the situation is resolved (settled or rendered determinate), has to discover and formulate the conditions which describe the problem at hand. For *they* are the conditions to be 'satisfied' and [are] the determinants of 'success.' Since these conditions are existential, they can be determined only by observational operations; the operational character of observation being clearly exhibited in the experimental character of all scientific determination of data. [ ] The conditions discovered, accordingly, in and by operational observation, constitute the *conditions of the problem* with which further inquiry is engaged; for the data, on this view, are always data of some specific problem and hence are not given ready-made to an inquiry but are determined in and by it. [ ] As the problem progressively assumes definite shape by means of repeated acts of observation, possible solutions suggest themselves. The process of reasoning is the elaboration of them.

When they are checked by reference to observed materials, they constitute the subject matter of inferential propositions. The latter are means of attaining the goal of knowledge as warranted assertion, not instances or examples of knowledge. They are also operational in nature since they institute new experimental observations whose subject matter provide both tests for old hypotheses and starting points for new ones or at least for modifying solutions previously entertained. And so on until a determinate situation is instituted."

13. Dewey, *Reconstruction in Philosophy*, p. xviii.

THE LEGITIMACY OF THE CONTEMPORARY

1. Weber, M. 1946. "Science as a Vocation," in *From Max Weber: Essays in Sociology*. Edited by H. Gerth and C. W. Mills. New York: Oxford University Press, p. 143. My gratitude to James Faubion and Tobias Rees.

2. Foucault, M. 1984. "What Is Enlightenment?" in *The Foucault Reader*. Edited by P. Rabinow. New York: Pantheon, p. 34.

3. Marquard, O. 1982. *Schwierigkeiten mit der Geschichtsphilosophie*. Frankfurt am Main: Suhrkamp Verlag.

4. *The Drosophila Genome. Science*, vol. 287, 24 March 2000. Although there is an excellent history of Drosophila genetics (Kohler, R. E. 1994. *Lords of the Fly: Drosophila Genetics and the Experimental Life*. Chicago: University of Chicago Press), it is not mentioned in the entire issue of *Science*.

5. Brenner, S. 2000. "The End of the Beginning." *Science* 287:2173.

6. Mullis's triumph was to move from the gene, à la Khoranna, to DNA.

7. Of the many books on this topic is Cook-Deegan, R. 1995. *The Gene Wars: Science, Politics, and the Human Genome Project*. New York: W. W. Norton.

8. Brenner, "The End of the Beginning," p. 2174.

9. Rubin, G. M., et al. 2000. "Comparative Genomics of the Eukaryotes." *Science* 287:2204–15. Drosophila melanogaster, Caenorhabditis elegans, Saccharomyces cervisiae. [Protein domains, (2) intracellular networks, (3) cell-cell interactions].

10. Ibid. (Haemophilus = 1425, Yeast = 4383 proteins, fly = 8065, worm = 9453).

11. Ibid; Warrick, J. M., et al. 1999. "Suppression of Polyglutamine-mediated Neurodegeneration in Drosophila by the Molecular Chaperone HSP70." *Nature Genetics* 23:425–28.

12. Habermas, J. 2003. *The Future of Human Nature*. Cambridge: Polity Press, p. 12.

13. Kant, I. 1949. *Fundamental Principles of the Metaphysic of Morals*. New York: Liberal Arts Press, p. 46.

14. Habermas, *The Future of Human Nature*, p. 12.

15. Canguilhem, G. 1976. "Nature dénaturée et nature naturante," in *Savoir, faire, espérer: les limites de la raison*. Bruxelles: Publications des Facultés Universitaires Saint-Louis, p. 71.

16. Hence Canguilhem would have equal scorn for those like Luc Ferry who reject ecology in the name of a neo-Kantian humanism that sacralizes the subject and humanity.

17. "Tels qui croient tenir un langage humaniste usent en fait d'un vocabulaire théologique. Scientifiquement parlant, dénaturation n'a pas de sens. Techniquement parlant, dénaturation signifie changement d'usage. Or, aucun usage d'une chose n'est inscrit dans la nature des choses. Le premier usage d'une chose est sa dénaturation."

18. "Il est certain qu'on ne dénature pas la nature en orientant ses pouvoirs d'effets qui ne lui sont pas ordinaires."

19. "Parce que la nature ne peut qu'être naturante, une nature dénaturée, à la fois fille et mère de la culture, est possible. Parce que cette dénaturation a du emprunter progressivement les voies de l'abstraction et de la représentation non-figurative qui sont celles de la science, et que de ce fait on n'a pas su reconnaître dans la nature dénaturée la nature naturante, une plainte et une colère sont nées, auxquelles la littérature et l'idéologie s'efforcent en vain de donner un poids philosophique." The second point: "Because nature can only be natural, a denatured nature, at one and the same time the mother and daughter of culture, is

possible. Because that denaturation progressively followed the path of abstraction or of nonfigurative representation which are those of science, and because of this fact one has failed to recognize 'la nature naturante dans la nature dénaturée,' complaint and anger have arisen, and literature and ideology have vainly sought to give these emotions some philosophic weight."

20. Luhmann, N. 1993. *Risk: A Sociological Theory*. New York: de Gruyter, p. 6.

21. "The Genome Sequence of Drosophila Melangaster": *Science* 287:2185–95.

23. Habermas, *The Future of Human Nature*, p. 15.

ADJACENCY

1. Weber, M. 1949. "'Objectivity' in Social Science and Social Policy," in *The Methodology of the Social Sciences*, pp. 49–112. New York: The Free Press.

2. Marcus, G. 2003. "On the Unbearable Slowness of Being an Anthropologist Now." *Xcp: Cross-cultural Poetics* 12:7; Bourdieu, P. 1990. "The Scholastic Point of View." *Cultural Anthropology* 5:380–91.

3. Even the historicization of the subject changes little in this respect because these same norms of patience and accuracy drive toward exhaustivity, and the rest are even more inscribed in the practice of historians.

4. Foucault, M. 1984. "Truth and Power," in *The Foucault Reader*. Edited by P. Rabinow, pp. 51–75. New York: Pantheon.

5. Nikolas Rose puts down "human." Personal communication.

6. Reardon, J. 2004. *Race to the Finish: Identity and Governance in an Age of Genomics*. Princeton: Princeton University Press.

7. For a sincere attempt to clarify the terms in this realm, and the unlikely prospects for success, see Sankar, P., and M. K. Cho. 2002. "Enhanced: Toward a New Vocabulary of Human Genetic Variation." *Science* 298:1337–38.

8. Rabinow, P. 1995. *French Modern: Norms and Forms of the Social Environment*, 2nd edition. Chicago: University of Chicago Press.

9. For example, Deleuze, G. 1968. *Différence et répétition*. Paris: Presses Universitaires de France, pp. 269ff.

OBSERVATION

1. James Faubion observes that Mead and Benedict thought psycho-analysis would help counter cultural prejudices and even more fundamentally would enable the uptake of the dreamlike Exotic Other into the fantasy world of one's own neurosis.

2. Koselleck, R. 2002. "On the Anthropological and Semantic Structure of *Bildung*," in *The Practice of Conceptual History: Timing History, Spacing Concepts*. Stanford: Stanford University Press.

3. Ibid., p. 173.

4. Although neither in French nor in English is there an exact equivalent of *Aufklärer*.

5. Ibid., p. 171. *Paideia* is another term related to these themes. Ibid., p. 192. And here we have another genealogical line that is eminently worth elaborating. It was Hegel in his *Philosophy of Right*, Koselleck points out, who claimed that all work is formative. Thus, *Bildung* cannot be defined by drawing a line between manual work and intellectual work. Self-formative work cannot be located by social markers or tags of distinction, nor can it be reduced to them. Rather, "work" refers to an occupation that mediates between particular abilities and tasks with the demands of the general public. Thus not all labor is work, and not all work is *Bildung*.

6. Comparisons are called for between Reinhart Koselleck's *Futures Past* and its analysis of how the past appears in modernity, and Michel Foucault's "What Is Enlightenment?" which queries the way the present appears in different historicities. Foucault is acute in showing how these questions lead to a problematization of modes of subjectivation, an issue that centrally concerns Luhmann, although he does not pose it in these terms. Koselleck, R. 1985. *Futures Past: On the Semantics of Historical Time*. Cambridge: MIT Press.

7. Luhmann always talks in terms of "society" as if it were a dynamic cybernetic system with no outside.

8. Luhmann, N. 1998. *Observations on Modernity*. Stanford: Stanford University Press, p. 63.

9. Ibid., p. 65.

10. The point about "perfection" is equally made by Deleuze and Guattari.

11. Ibid., p. 66.

12. Koselleck, *Futures Past*.

13. Pence, G. 1998. *Who's Afraid of Human Cloning?* Lanham: Rowman and Littlefield.

14. On encyclopedias, see MacIntyre, A. 1990. *Three Rival Versions of Moral Enquiry: Encyclopedia, Genealogy and Tradition*. Notre Dame: Notre Dame University Press.

15. Thanks to James Faubion for this phrase.

16. Luhmann, *Observations on Modernity*, p. 93. See Edward Andrew on value as subjectivation. 1995. *The Genealogy of Values: The Aesthetic Economy of Nietzsche and Proust*. Lanham: Rowman and Littlefield.

17. See Rabinow, *Anthropos Today*.

18. Luhmann, *Observations on Modernity*, p. 3.

19. Hegel, G.W.F. 1988. *Introduction to the Philosophy of History*. Indianapolis: Hackett Publishing Company, p. 5.

20. Ibid., pp. 3–5.

21. Thucydides, ed. 1996. *The Peloponnesian War*. Vol. 1. *The Landmark Thucydides*. New York: The Free Press, p. 1.

22. James Faubion has been helpful and generous in providing help with the Greek text as well as its meaning.

23. 1.22.1–3: Cogan translation.

24. Cogan, M. 1981. *The Human Thing: The Speeches and Principles of Thucydides' History*. Chicago: University of Chicago Press.

25. Ibid., p. xv.

26. Ibid., p. xvii.

VEHEMENT CONTEMPORARIES

1. Brown, P. 2002. *Poverty and Leadership in the Later Roman Empire*. Hanover, NH: University Press of New England, p. 1.

2. Trilling, L. 1971. *Sincerity and Authenticity*. Cambridge: Harvard University Press, pp. 5–6.

3. Ibid., p. 9.

4. Ibid., p. 1.

5. Clifford, J. 1988. *The Predicament of Culture*. Cambridge: Harvard University Press.

6. See James Faubion's illuminating work on this topic.

7. Memmi, D. 1996. *Les gardiens du corps. Dix ans de magistère bioéthique*. Paris: Éditions de L'École des Hautes Études en Sciences Sociales; Badiou, A. 1993. *L'éthique. Essai sur la conscience du Mal*. Paris: Hatier. Marilyn Strathern has pointed to the need for "society" as a

counterpoint to the scientific institutions. Without society there could be no responsible interlocutor.

8. Shreeve, J. 2004. *The Genome War: How Craig Venter Tried to Capture the Code of Life and Save the World*. New York: Alfred A. Knopf, p. 237.

9. Ibid., p. 138.

10. Ibid., p. 376.

11. Sulston, J., and G. Ferry. 2001. *The Common Thread. A Story of Science, Politics, Ethics, and the Human Genome*. Washington, DC: John Henry Press.

12. Shreeve, *The Genome War*, p. 193.

13. Ibid., p. 48.

14. Ibid., p. 280.

15. Ibid., p. 124.

16. Ibid., p. 134.

17. Ibid., p. 289.

18. Cogan, *The Human Thing*.

19. Nussbaum, M. 1994. *The Therapy of Desire: Theory and Practice in Hellenistic Ethics*. Princeton: Princeton University Press.

20. In Trilling, *Sincerity and Authenticity*, p. 108.

21. For a classicist account, see Harris, W. V. 2001. *Restraining Rage. The Ideology of Anger Control in Classical Antiquity*. Cambridge: Harvard University Press; Huart, P. 1968. *L'Analyse du vocabulaire psychologique dans l'oeuvre de Thucydide*. Paris: Librairie Klincksieck.

22. Plato. 1961. *The Republic*. Princeton: Princeton University Press, Bollingen Series, p. 680.

23. "Gentleness is the observance of the mean in relation to anger. There is as a matter of fact no recognized name for the mean in this respect—indeed, there can hardly be said to be names for the extremes either—so we apply the word gentleness to the mean though really it inclines to the side of the defect. This has no name, but the excess may be called a sort of irascibility" (4, v, 1–2). "The defect, on the other hand, call it a sort of Lack of Spirit or whatnot, is blamed; since those who do not get angry at things at which it is right to be angry are considered foolish, and so are those who do not get angry in the right manner, at the right time, and with the right people" (5, v, 5). Gentleness—*praotes*. Anger—*orge*. Lack of spirit—*aorgesia*.

24. Fukuyama, F. 1992. *The End of History and the Last Man*. New York: The Free Press. And this via Alexandre Kojève.

25. Fisher, P. 2002. *The Vehement Passions*. Princeton: Princeton University Press, p. 4.

26. Elias, N. 1983. *The Court Society*. Oxford: Blackwell; Sloterdijk, P. 1999. *Regeln für den Menschenpark. Ein Antwortschreiben zu Heideggers Brief über den Humanismus*. Frankfurt am Main: Suhrkamp Verlag; Sloterdijk, P. 2001. *Das Menschentreibhaus. Stichworte zur historischen und prophetischen Anthropologie*. Weimar: VDG.

27. Fisher, *The Vehement Passions*, p. 177.

28. Ibid., p. 101 (Ethics, 7.7).

29. Williams, R. 1977. *Marxism and Literature*. Oxford: Oxford University Press.

30. MacIntyre, A. 1990. *Three Rival Versions of Moral Enquiry: Encyclopedia, Genealogy and Tradition*. South Bend: Notre Dame University Press.

31. Foucault, M. 2001. *L'herméneutique du sujet. Cours au Collège de France, 1981–1982*. Paris: Gallimard/Seuil.

32. Fisher, *The Vehement Passions*, p. 1.

MARKING TIME: GERHARD RICHTER

1. Carlo Caduff provided the material and the initial version of this entire section and graciously agreed to let me modify and use it for different purposes. Haftmann, W. 1950. *Paul Klee. Wege bildnerischen Denkens*. München: Prestel Verlag, p. 89; Klee, P. 1998. *Théorie de l'art moderne*. Paris Gallimard, p. 28. "Peut-être est-il philosophe à son insu, et s'il ne tient pas, comme les optimistes, ce monde pour le meilleure des mondes possibles, ni ne veut affirmer non plus que celui qui nous entoure est trop mauvais pour qu'on puisse le prendre comme modèle, il se dit toutefois sous cette forme reçue, il n'est pas le seul monde possible."

2. Haftmann, *Paul Klee*, p. 93. "Führen Sie Ihre Schüler zur Natur, in die Natur! Lassen Sie sie erleben, wie sich eine Knospe bildet, wie ein Baum wächst, wie sich ein Falter auftut, damit sie ebenso reich werden, ebenso beweglich, ebenso eigensinnig wie die grosse Natur."

3. Ibid.

4. Ibid., p. 90. "Namen könnten sich einstellen, die wir diesen Dingen geben möchten mehr als Gleichnis aus der Biologie denn als Bezeichnung."

5. Klee, *Théorie de l'art moderne*, p. 10.

6. Haftmann, *Paul Klee*, p. 90. "Es ist eine Natur, die eben gerade nur ein wenig weiter als üblich ist."

7. Klee, *Théorie de l'art moderne*, p. 28. "L'artiste n'accorde pas aux apparences de la nature la même importance contraignante que ses nombreux détracteurs réalistes. Il ne s'y sent pas tellement assujetti, les formes arrêtées ne représentant pas à ses yeux l'essence du processus créateur dans la nature. La nature naturante lui importe davantage que la nature naturée."

8. Ibid., p. 29.

9. Hoppe-Sailer, R. 2003. "Organismes/Art—Les racines historiques de l'art biotech," in *L'Art biotech*. Edited by J. Hauser. Nantes: Editions le lieu unique, p. 89.

10. Cited in Hauser: "Fonder une science nouvelle qui montrerait comment les formes et des schémas naturels peuvent être transposés sans grands difficulté dans une production humain."

11. Gedrim, R. J. 1993. "Edward Steichen's 1936 Exhibition of Delphinium Blooms: An Art of Flower Breeding. *"History of Photography"* 17:356.

12. Ibid., p. 352.

13. Ibid., p. 356.

14. Ibid., p. 357.

15. Chevrier, J.-F. 2000. "Between the Fine Arts and the Media," in *Photography and Painting in the Work of Gerhard Richter: Four Essays on Atlas*. Barcelona: Libres de Recerca, pp. 35, 45.

16. As it is expensive to include plates from a living artist, none is reproduced here. A selection of Richter images is available at www.gerhard-richter.com. Thus, Richter's most prolific commentator, Benjamin Buchloh, to whom Richter has accorded a series of extended interviews over the years, and who has attempted to find a coherent and contestatory thematic in Richter's work, has been directly repudiated by Richter time and time again. Nonetheless, Buchloh has continued his search.

17. Storr, R. 2002. *Gerhard Richter: Forty Years of Painting*. New York: Museum of Modern Art, p. 172.

18. Deleuze, G., and F. Guattari. 1996. *What Is Philosophy?* New York: Columbia University Press, p. 176. "Art does not have opinions. Art undoes the triple organization of perceptions, affects, and opinions in order to substitute a monument composed of percepts, affects, and blocs of sensations that take the place of language."

19. Osborne, P. 2001. "Images abstraites. Signe, image et l'esthé-

tique dans la peinture de Gerhard Richter." *Le Part de l'Oeil* 17–18:228–39. I would like to thank Peter Osborne for his generosity in sharing his work and idea with me.

20. Storr, *Gerhard Richter*, p. 109.

21. Osborne, "Images abstraites."

22. Richter, G. 1995. *The Daily Practice of Painting: Writings 1962–93*. Cambridge: MIT Press, p. 124.

23. Chevrier, "Between the Fine Arts and the Media," p. 42.

24. Ibid., p. 41.

25. Richter, *The Daily Practice of Painting*, p. 11.

26. Chevrier, "Between the Fine Arts and the Media," p. 35.

27. Ibid., p. 45.

28. Ibid., p. 37.

29. Storr, *Gerhard Richter*, p. 168.

30. Chevrier, "Between the Fine Arts and the Media," p. 94.

31. Storr, *Gerhard Richter*, p. 169.

32. Chevrier, "Between the Fine Arts and the Media," p. 33. "Photography was a way of introducing existential content—direct, immediate, and also very common—into a pictorial rhetoric too exclusively centered on either the subjective resonances of gesture and material, or the idealization of geometric construction."

33. Ibid., p. 35.

34. Ibid., p. 55, note 22.

35. Richter, *The Daily Practice of Painting*, p. 113.

36. Ibid., May 30, 1990.

37. Clark, T. J. 1999. *Farewell to an Idea. Episodes from a History of Modernism*. New Haven: Yale University Press.

38. Osborne, P. 1992. "Painting Negation: Gerhard Richter's Negatives." *October* 62:111–12.

39. Ibid., p. 106.

40. Ibid., p. 109.

41. Ibid.

42. Ibid., p. 110.

43. "Having taken color charts and photo-enlargement as his first two jumping-off points on the way to abstraction, Richter then tried a third, which he called Inpainting. [. . .] The Inpaintings are the often uningratiating purposely muddled extensions of the clean and orderly Color Charts." Storr, R. 2003. *Gerhard Richter: Doubt and Belief in Painting*. New York: The Museum of Modern Art, p. 92.

44. Ibid., p. 111.

45. Gandy, M. 1997. "Contradictory Modernities: Conceptions of Nature in the Art of Joseph Bueys and Gerhard Richter." *Annals of the Association of American Geographers* 87:648.

46. Danto, A. C. 1998. *After the End of Art*. Princeton: Princeton University Press; Michaud, Y. 2004. *L'art à l'état gazeux*. Paris: Hachette Littérature.

47. Butin H., and S. Gronert, eds. 2004. *Gerhard Richter: Editions 1965–2004: Catalogue Raisonné*. Stuttgart: Hatje Cantz Publishers.

48. Osborne, "Images abstraites."

49. Manovich, L. 2001. *The Language of the New Media*. Cambridge: MIT Press.

50. Christopher Kelty has provided invaluable insight and clarification for this discussion of the new media.

51. Manovich, *The Language of the New Media*, p. 126.

52. Kelty (personal communication).

53. Klee, P. 1968. *Pedagogical Sketchbook*. New York: Faber & Faber.

54. Manovich, *The Language of the New Media*, p. 131.

55. Ibid., p. 125.

56. Bolter, J. D., and R. Grusin. 1999. *Remediation: Understanding New Media*. Cambridge: MIT Press, p. 89.

✳

BIBLIOGRAPHY

Andrew, E. 1995. *The Genealogy of Values. The Aesthetic Economy of Nietzsche and Proust*. Lanham: Rowman and Littlefield.

Badiou, A. 1993. *L'éthique. Essai sur la conscience du Mal*. Paris: Hatier.

Blumenberg, H. 1983. *The Legitimacy of the Modern Age*. Translated by R. M. Wallace. Cambridge: MIT Press.

Bolter, J. D., and R. Grusin. 1999. *Remediation. Understanding New Media*. Cambridge: MIT Press.

Bourdieu, P. 1990. "The Scholastic Point of View." *Cultural Anthropology* 5:380–91.

Brenner, S. 2000. "The End of the Beginning." *Science* 287:2173–74.

Brown, P. 2002. *Poverty and Leadership in the Later Roman Empire*. Hanover: University Press of New England.

Butin, H., and S. Gronert, eds. 2004. *Gerhard Richter. Editions 1965–2004: Catalogue Raisonné*. Stuttgart: Hatje Cantz Publishers.

Canguilhem, G. 1976. "Nature dénaturée et nature naturante," in *Savoir, faire, espérer: les limites de la raison*. Bruxelles: Publications des Facultés Universitaires Saint-Louis.

Chevrier, J.-F. 2000. "Between the Fine Arts and the Media," in *Photography and Painting in the Work of Gerhard Richter: Four Essays on Atlas*. Barcelona: Libres de Recerca.

Clark, T. J. 1999. *Farewell to an Idea: Episodes from a History of Modernism*. New Haven: Yale University Press.

Clifford, J. 1988. *The Predicament of Culture*. Cambridge: Harvard University Press.

Cogan, M. 1981. *The Human Thing: The Speeches and Principles of Thucydides' History*. Chicago: University of Chicago Press.

Collier, S. J., A. Lakoff, and P. Rabinow. 2004. "Biosecurity: Towards an Anthropology of the Contemporary." *Anthropology Today* 20:3–7.

Cook-Deegan, R. 1995. *The Gene Wars: Science, Politics, and the Human Genome Project*. New York: W. W. Norton.

Danto, A. C. 1998. *After the End of Art*. Princeton: Princeton University Press.

Delanda, M. 2004. *Intensive Science and Virtual Philosophy*. London: Continuum.

Deleuze, G. 1968. *Différence et répétition*. Paris: Presses Universitaires de France.

Deleuze, G., and F. Guattari. 1996. *What Is Philosophy?* New York: Columbia University Press.

Dewey, J. 1948. *Reconstruction in Philosophy*. Boston: Beacon Press.

——. 1991. *Logic. The Theory of Inquiry*. Vol. 12. *The Later Works, 1925–38*. Carbondale: Southern Illinois Press.

Elias, N. 1983. *The Court Society*. Oxford: Blackwell.

Fisher, P. 2002. *The Vehement Passions*. Princeton: Princeton University Press.

Foucault, M. 1984. "Truth and Power," in *The Foucault Reader*. Edited by P. Rabinow, pp. 51–75. New York: Pantheon.

——. 1984. "What Is Enlightenment?" in *The Foucault Reader*. Edited by P. Rabinow. New York: Pantheon.

——. 1997. "What Is Enlightenment?" in *Ethics: Subjectivity and Truth, Essential Works of Foucault 1954–1984*, pp. 303–19. New York: The New Press.

——. 2001. *L'herméneutique du sujet. Cours au Collège de France, 1981–1982*. Paris: Gallimard / Seuil.

Fukuyama, F. 1992. *The End of History and the Last Man*. New York: The Free Press.

Gandy, M. 1997. "Contradictory Modernities: Conceptions of Nature in the Art of Joseph Bueys and Gerhard Richter." *Annals of the Association of American Geographers* 87:636–59.

Gedrim, R. J. 1993. "Edward Steichen's 1936 Exhibition of Delphinium Blooms: An Art of Flower Breeding." *History of Photography* 17:352–63.

Habermas, J. 2003. *The Future of Human Nature*. Cambridge: Polity Press.

Haftmann, W. 1950. *Paul Klee. Wege bildnerischen Denkens*. München: Prestel Verlag.

Harris, W. V. 2001. *Restraining Rage: The Ideology of Anger Control in Classical Antiquity*. Cambridge: Harvard University Press.

Hegel, G. W. F. 1988. *Introduction to the Philosophy of History*. Indianapolis: Hackett Publishing Company.

Hoppe-Sailer, R. 2003. "Organismes/Art—Les racines historiques de l'art biotech," in *L'Art biotech*. Edited by J. Hauser. Nantes: Editions le lieu unique.

Huart, P. 1968. *L'Analyse du vocabulaire psycholoqigue dans l'oeuvre de Thucydide*. Paris: Librairie Klincksieck.

Kant, I. 1949. *Fundamental Principles of the Metaphysic of Morals*. New York: Liberal Arts Press.

Klee, P. 1968. *Pedagogical Sketchbook*. New York: Faber & Faber.

———. 1998. *Théorie de l'art moderne*. Paris: Gallimard.

Kohler, R. E. 1994. *Lords of the Fly: Drosophila Genetics and the Experimental Life*. Chicago: University of Chicago Press.

Koselleck, R. 1985. *Futures Past: On the Semantics of Historical Time*. Cambridge: MIT Press.

———. 2002. "On the Anthropological and Semantic Structure of Bildung," in *The Practice of Conceptual History: Timing History, Spacing Concepts*. Stanford: Stanford University Press.

Luhmann, N. 1993. *Risk: A Sociological Theory*. New York: de Gruyter.

———. 1998. *Observations on Modernity*. Stanford: Stanford University Press.

MacIntyre, A. 1990. *Three Rival Versions of Moral Enquiry. Encyclopedia, Genealogy and Tradition*. Notre Dame: Notre Dame University Press.

Manovich, L. 2001. *The Language of the New Media*. Cambridge: MIT Press.

Marcus, G. 2003. "On the Unbearable Slowness of Being an Anthropologist Now." *Xcp: Cross-cultural Poetics* 12:7–20.

Marquard, O. 1982. *Schwierigkeiten mit der Geschichtsphilosophie*. Frankfurt am Main: Suhrkamp Verlag.

Memmi, D. 1996. *Les gardiens du corps. Dix ans de magistère bioéthique*. Paris: Éditions de l'École des Hautes Études en Sciences sociales.

Michaud, Y. 2004. *L'art à l'état gazeux*. Paris: Hachette Littérature.

Nietzsche, F. 1995. *Unpublished Writings from the Period of Unfashionable Observations*. Stanford: Stanford University Press.

Nussbaum, M. 1994. *The Therapy of Desire: Theory and Practice in Hellenistic Ethics*. Princeton: Princeton University Press.

Osborne, P. 1992. "Painting Negation: Gerhard Richter's Negatives." *October* 62:102–13.

———. 2001. "Images abstraites. Signe, image et l'esthétique dans la peinture de Gerhard Richter." *Le Part de l'Oeil* 17–18:228–39.

Pauly, P. 1987. *Controlling Life: Jacques Loeb and the Engineering Ideal in Biology*. Oxford: Oxford University Press.

Pence, G. 1998. *Who's Afraid of Human Cloning?* Lanham: Rowman and Littlefield.

Plato. 1961. *The Republic*. Princeton: Bollingen Series.

Rabinow, P. 1975. *Symbolic Domination: Cultural Form and Historical Change in Morocco*. Chicago: University of Chicago Press.

——. 1995. *French Modern: Norms and Forms of the Social Environment*, 2nd edition. Chicago: University of Chicago Press.

——. 1996. *Making PCR: A Story of Biotechnology*. Chicago: University of Chicago Press.

——. 1999. *French DNA: Trouble in Purgatory*. Chicago: University of Chicago Press.

——. 2003. *Anthropos Today: Reflections on Modern Equipment*. Princeton: Princeton University Press.

Rabinow, P., and T. Dan-Cohen. 2006. *A Machine to Make a Future: Biotech Chronicles*. 2nd edition. Princeton: Princeton University Press.

Reardon, J. 2004. *Race to the Finish: Identity and Governance in an Age of Genomics*. Princeton: Princeton University Press.

Richter, G. 1995. *The Daily Practice of Painting: Writings 1962–93*. Cambridge: MIT Press.

Rubin, G. M., et al. 2000. "Comparative Genomics of the Eukaryotes." *Science* 287:2204–15.

Ryan, A. 1995. *John Dewey and the High Tide of American Liberalism*. New York: Norton.

Sankar, P., and M. K. Cho. 2002. "Enhanced: Toward a New Vocabulary of Human Genetic Variation." *Science* 298:1337–38.

Shreeve, J. 2004. *The Genome War: How Craig Venter Tried to Capture the Code of Life and Save the World*. New York: Alfred A. Knopf.

Sloterdijk, P. 1999. *Regeln für den Menschenpark. Ein Antwortschreiben zu Heideggers Brief über den Humanismus*. Frankfurt am Main: Suhrkamp Verlag.

——. 2001. *Das Menschentreibhaus. Stichworte zur historischen und prophetischen Anthropologie*. Weimar: VDG.

Storr, R. 2002. *Gerhard Richter. Forty Years of Painting* New York: The Museum of Modern Art.

——. 2003. *Gerhard Richter. Doubt and Belief in Painting*. New York: The Museum of Modern Art.

Sulston, J., and G. Ferry. 2001. *The Common Thread: A Story of Science, Politics, Ethics, and the Human Genome*. Washington, DC: John Henry Press.

Thucydides. Editor. 1996. *The Peloponnesian War*. Vol. 1. *The Landmark Thucydides*. New York: The Free Press.

Trilling, L. 1971. *Sincerity and Authenticity*. Cambridge: Harvard University Press.

Warrick, J. M., H. Y. E. Chan, G. L. Gray-Board, Y. Chai, H. L. Paulson, and N. M. Bonini. 1999. "Suppression of Polyglutamine-mediated Neurodegeneration in Drosophila by the Molecular Chaperone HSP70." *Nature Genetics* 23:425–28.

Weber, M. 1946. "Science as a Vocation," in *From Max Weber: Essays in Sociology*. Edited by H. Gerth and C. W. Mills. New York: Oxford University Press.

———. 1949. "'Objectivity' in Social Science and Social Policy," in *The Methodology of the Social Sciences*, pp. 49–112. New York: The Free Press.

Williams, R. 1977. *Marxism and Literature*. Oxford: Oxford University Press.

INDEX

Open reading frame — (17)